When Faith
and
Decisions
Collide

When Faith
and
Decisions
Collide

FINDING GOD'S WILL

FOR YOUR LIFE

Dan Schaeffer

Discovery House Publishers

Books, music, and videos that feed the soul with the Word of God

Box 3566 Grand Rapids, MI 49501

I dedicate this book to my family:

ANNETTE, CHRISTI, ANDREW, AND KATIE.

*Being husband and dad in this family is more fun
than one man should be allowed to have.
Thanks for being patient and understanding.*

This book was previously published by Discovery House as *The Bush Won't Burn, and
I'm All Out of Matches: How to Find the Will of God When You've Looked Everywhere.*

Discovery House Publishers is affiliated with RBC Ministries,
Grand Rapids, Michigan.

Discovery House books are distributed to the trade exclusively by
Barbour Publishing, Inc., Uhrichsville, Ohio.

Requests for permission to quote from this book should be directed to: Permissions
Department, Discovery House Publishers, P O Box 3566, Grand Rapids, MI 49501.

Unless otherwise indicated, Scripture quotations are from the New
American Standard Bible. Copyright © 1960, 1962, 1968, 1971, 1972, 1973,
1975, 1977, 1995. The Lockman Foundation. Used by permission.

Library of Congress Cataloging-in-Publication Data
Schaeffer, Daniel, 1958–
    When faith and decisions collide : finding God's will for your life / Daniel
    Schaeffer.— [Rev. ed.].
        p. cm.
    Rev. ed. of: The bush won't burn, and I'm all out of matches.
    Includes bibliographical references.
    ISBN 1-57293-164-7
    1. God—Will. 2. Christian life—Evangelical Free Church authors. 3. Schaeffer,
    Daniel, 1958– I. Schaeffer, Daniel, 1958– Bush won't burn, and I'm all out of
    matches. II. Title.
    BV4501.3.S345 2005
    248.4'8995—dc22   2005013217

Printed in the United States of America
06 07 08 09 10 / CHG / 10 9 8 7 6 5 4 3 2

CONTENTS

INTRODUCTION

And the Search Goes On

Life can be funny, in a really annoying kind of way. Consider the case of Bobo (Alva) Holloman's unique achievement: pitching a no-hitter in his first major-league start—and then never pitching so much as one more complete game for the rest of his career.

Yes, on May 6, 1953, Bobo blanked the Philadelphia A's 6–0 on behalf of the normally hapless St. Louis Browns. It wasn't even a terribly well-pitched game. Every time one of the A's hit the ball, there was, miraculously, a Brownie there to catch it.

Bobo, naturally, didn't see his accomplishment as the fluke it was. He and his wife even wrote a book, *This One and That One,* to tell us the story. Bobo never came close to that level of performance again. He finished the season—and his major league career—with a truly unremarkable 3–7 record.

Or consider the case of the jungle natives in the Second World War. During the war, the logistics of supplies in the Pacific Theater were complicated by the fact that U.S. pilots had to fly long distances over open water. Cargo planes were often forced to crash-land, or simply crash, on remote islands, some inhabited by natives who had never seen an airplane up close, much less the stuff we Americans packed into one: food in cans, ready-made clothes, radios, medicine. After the war this phenomenon ended. But the hope did not.

A kind of religion grew up: the "cargo cult." Believers worshiped the big metal birds—those that were rusting away in the jungle, and those that flew overhead—praying they would crash and bestow their magical cargoes on them again. They never did.

And lastly there is the story of the young couple who brought home a puppy and let him out in the backyard to play. The puppy soon spied a baby squirrel and chased the squirrel up a tree. The puppy sat at the foot of the tree and barked and barked. The baby squirrel, unnerved, attempted to jump to the branch of another tree. It missed the branch and fell straight into the mouth of the astonished barking puppy.

For the next fifteen years, until the day he died, the dog sat under the same tree in the same spot, waiting for another squirrel to fall from the sky into his waiting jaws. It never happened.[1] Signs are hard to figure sometimes. We think we know what they mean, but what happens when they don't turn out to mean what we thought? We are a sign-conscious people, constantly looking for them to determine what to do next. As Christians, we are also sign-watchers, albeit sanctified sign-watchers. We're constantly looking for signs to tell us what God's will is, or will be, or was, or could be. Well, let's just say there's a lot of confusion surrounding the whole subject of God's will.

Some of our misunderstandings about how to find God's will lead to amusing stories; some of them lead to tears. But in both cases we can become frustrated trying to "find" the will of God.

There are some very famous searches in history. The search for the fountain of youth, the search for Noah's ark, the search for the mother lode, the search for the missing link, and the search for the missing sock. But few things seem to be more pressing on the minds of Christians than the search for God's will for their lives.

Where is God leading me, how can I know, and what are the signs? Far from being an academic question, this issue is painfully practical. We are faced with a seemingly infinite number of choices in life, of which we can choose only a few. Just picking out toothpaste can be mind-boggling. I relate to the man in the commercial who is asked whether he wants paper or plastic for his groceries. All of a sudden, all the issues of recycling, deforestation, and landfills come to a head; he gets a case of brain overload and he freezes, unable to answer.

As Christians, we know that God wants to lead us and guide us. We also know that the choices we make often impact our life's direction, so they are terribly significant. So our reasoning is simple: just get God involved in the decision-making loop. It sounds like a simple process, like deciding between paper and plastic.

Unfortunately, this is precisely where the problems usually begin. Everyone seems to have a different method for determining God's will for his or her life, and ours! Some tell us just to trust our feelings, while others pass along verses of Scripture that "had your name on them." Still others reduce the will of God to a simple formula of one, two, three, four; others are busy laying out fleeces (when they can find one).

While some claim success, the results often leave us less than confident that this is "the method." People who have used these or other methods believed they would ultimately understand God's will; they chased it doggedly, only to find disappointment at the end of the mirage. I empathize, because I've seen the same mirage. I have used all of the above methods, plus a few I won't name out of sheer embarrassment. But at all times I was sincerely seeking the will of God for my life. What I can joke about now was no joke at the time.

At stake is more than just finding the elusive will of God for my life. I have spent many hours counseling with severely disappointed and disillusioned Christians who feel God either led them on or let them down. More is involved now than just finding the will of God, for to them the character of God has come into question. Hurt and deeply disappointed, their belief in God's goodness, mercy, and care has been dashed.

And to that issue, this book is dedicated. There will be no easy answers, no guaranteed formulas, for we will be looking at God's will from a different vantage point. We will look at the will of God *as a journey*, rather than a destination; something to walk in, rather than just seek out. I hope we will discover that the search for God's will for our lives entails more than just telling us when to turn right or left, buy or sell, become an accountant or a plumber.

My greatest desire for this book, and you who read it, is that it may play some part in healing wounds of disappointment and discouragement. God has not been playing cat-and-mouse games with you, nor is He inattentive or uncaring concerning the details of your life. In fact, it is my prayer that you will understand the love and involvement of God toward you at a deeper level than ever before.

With that in mind, let the search continue.

> The will of God—
> Nothing more, nothing less.
>
> —G. Campbell Morgan[2]

FOLLOW THROUGH

1. If I could ask God one question concerning His will for my life right now, it would be

2. The approach I have used in the past to determine the will of God for my life is

3. How satisfied am I with my present approach to finding God's will? (Circle one and explain why.)

   Greatly   Mostly   Fairly   Hardly

4. I identify most with: (Explain why.)

   Bobo Holloman—

The jungle natives—

The puppy with the squirrel—

5. How sign-conscious do I seem to be? Give an example.

6. I believe God is involved in my decision-making loop ___% of the time. (Explain.)

Making Contact

Write down on a piece of paper what you most need to get out of this study. Make it a personal letter to God, sharing honestly your doubts, frustrations, concerns, and hopes. Share this letter with others in your group.

If your letter is too personal, just share the general thrust of the letter. Keep this letter handy, and invite others in your group to pray with you concerning your goals. At the end of the study, note how many of your questions God has answered, how many He has yet to answer, and the importance of the questions that remain.

CHAPTER ONE

The Rearview Mirror of Life

When I was younger, I worked for a year as a driver for a company in southern California. I delivered parts from our company to other companies in the area. This involved relying on maps and addresses, as I was often driving through unfamiliar territory.

Invariably I would be driving down a street at the speed limit of thirty-five or forty miles per hour, trying to spot the address on the side of a building or street curb. If I slowed down to see better, the traffic behind me would slow down and I would be the object of blaring horns. I always went as slow as I dared, but occasionally I would realize, after looking back and forth from one side of the street to the other, that I had actually passed my destination. When that happened I had to quickly glance in my rearview mirror and try to spot the building.

I have come to the conclusion that this is often the only way we can correctly perceive some aspects of God's will—in the rearview mirror of life.

I was thinking about this recently when we invited some Christian friends over for dinner. As we finished dinner we began talking about our backgrounds, and some of the traumatic and difficult experiences we had encountered in life.

As we shared experiences we had lived through twenty and thirty years ago, and how hard and unwanted they had been at the time, we began to realize how significantly these experiences had impacted our lives in a positive way. What we couldn't begin to see at the time was our immaturity, wrong ideas about God and life, and attitudes that desperately needed to be changed. At the time the experiences seemed overwhelming and designed to destroy us. There was no way, we realized years later, that we could have expected to understand what God was doing through these events.

But in retrospect it made sense to us. Though none of us would want to repeat those moments again, we all agreed that they had been necessary for our growth. The pain and difficulty had transformed us in a way nothing else could. But only from the rearview mirror of life could we see that. The will of God had involved pain, but not for pain's sake. There was a loving, caring, and wise purpose behind it all.

Paul Tournier wrote, "God leads us step by step, from event to event. Only afterwards, as we look back over the way we have come and reconsider certain important moments in our lives in the light of all that has followed them, or when we survey the whole progress of our lives, do we experience the feeling of having been led without knowing it, the feeling that God has mysteriously guided us."[3]

LIFE WITHOUT A MAP

I flew over vast areas of our country in my father's private plane when I was younger, but when I see those same areas from ground level, my perspective about them changes dramatically. Seeing a mountain from 10,000 feet isn't the same as standing on it. The tree at 10,000 feet isn't nearly as clear as the tree you can see from your car.

I want to begin this subject of the will of God by touching immediately on an immensely important issue: the need to come to terms with the fact that God sometimes doesn't reveal His will to us until the future has become the past. At times we will have no idea what is going on in our lives; only in retrospect will we clearly see that God has been leading us according to His sovereign will.

This means that sometimes God's sovereign providential for our lives is something He will not tell us about. No instructions will be forthcoming. His Spirit leads us, His revealed moral will and biblical principles guide us—but alas, the information we most seek will be withheld. At least, at the time, that's the way it will seem.

We will want clear and definitive information to assure us that we are making the right decision and heading in the right direction. But sometimes that doesn't happen. Wanting a meal we will need to be content with an appetizer. Our hunger for information will not be satisfied. We will instead be given only enough information to make the next small baby-step.

As a result, we'll sometimes have to make decisions with precious little information, without knowing how those decisions will pan out. And here we learn a valuable lesson. This very struggle to discern the will of God for our lives is part of God's will.

There are times when only from the rearview mirror of life will our experiences and God's leading in them come into clear focus. Only then will we discover that what we fought against, complained about, tried desperately to escape from, was absolutely necessary for our maturing in Christ. Sir Thomas Browne concurred, saying, "There are in everyone's life certain connections, twists, and turns which pass awhile under the category of chance, but at the last, well examined, prove to be the very hand of God."[4]

CALL ME MANASSEH

One of my favorite characters in the Bible is Joseph. Later in his life, Joseph has two sons born to him in Egypt, during a time when he is ruling for Pharaoh.

> Joseph named the firstborn Manasseh, "For," he said, "God has made me forget all my trouble and all my father's household." He named the second Ephraim, "For," he said, "God has made me fruitful in the land of my affliction" (Genesis 41:51–52).

I relate at a very deep level to what Joseph says. I had a very difficult home life for many years, and at times it seemed as though God was determined to find out how much trouble I could take.

But more than thirty years later, I can echo with Joseph, "God has made me forget all my trouble and all my father's household."

Furthermore, I think I can shed some light on his words. Joseph was not saying that he couldn't remember his past difficulties; he remembered them clearly enough, but his past was no longer the focus of his life.

Yes, Joseph's life had been difficult, even tragic, for long, long stretches. He had been the victim of sibling jealousy, sold into slavery by his brothers who kept the vile deed from their father. Bought by an Egyptian army officer and taken to Egypt, he proved himself a faithful and able steward for the man. Unfortunately, the man's wife made continual sexual advances toward Joseph, which he rebuffed at every turn.

Jilted, the wife then falsely accused Joseph of rape, for which he was thrown into prison by his master. From bad to worse. Again, in prison his abilities are noticed and he comes into contact with two of Pharaoh's trusted advisors who had fallen into their ruler's disfavor. One of them has a dream which Joseph correctly interprets, and the advisor is brought back into Pharaoh's favor as Joseph had predicted.

However, even though the advisor promised to remember Joseph before Pharaoh and plead for him, he didn't. At this point Joseph could not have been surprised. Nothing had been going his way—for a long, long time, even though he had been faithful and honest.

Several more years go by and Joseph languishes in prison until finally Pharaoh has a disturbing dream which no one can interpret. Only then does the advisor remember Joseph, the "dream teller" in prison. From then on things start to go right, but remember, for many, many years Joseph's life went from bad to worse to unbelievable—which makes his statement all the more startling.

He was not controlled by his past, it did not haunt him. It, in fact, had been the very instrument God used to bring him to such a place of blessedness that his troubles could finally be put into perspective.

From the rearview mirror of life, Joseph could finally see what God had been doing. He saw now the purpose behind the difficult experiences he had been required to endure. "God has made me fruitful in the land of my affliction." Note the word *fruitful*. There was more to Joseph's life, he came to realize, than his perceived need for personal peace and comfort. He was to be a tool that God would use to keep thousands upon thousands, perhaps millions, of people alive. And among those thousands he was destined to save was his own beloved, though less than loving, family.

But when, we have to ask ourselves, did he come to this conclusion? Was it when he was thrown into the pit by his brothers? Did he understand God's will and work in his life then? Did God's will for his life suddenly come into focus when he hit bottom?

Was it when he was sold into slavery? On that long dreary march to Egypt, with a lifetime of slavery to look forward to, his brothers behind him counting the money they had gotten for him, his father grieving over his supposed death, did the will of God for his life suddenly become clear? Did he say, "Oh, now I see what God wants for the rest of my life! What a clever plan *this* is!"?

Was it when Potiphar's wife accused him of rape, prompting Potiphar to throw him in prison? Can we picture Joseph humming, "God Is So Good," to himself as he is thrown into a dungeon?

Was it when he interpreted the dreams of Pharaoh's trusted advisors in prison, and in gratitude was completely forgotten? As he languished several more years in prison, was he using that time to pick out the names Ephraim and Manasseh for his future children? Somehow I doubt it.

Yet, eventually, Joseph is promoted and becomes Pharaoh's right-hand man; he is responsible for all the affairs of the nation. At just that time along come his brothers from their home where famine has struck; the very same brothers who had started him off on the "good life" he was to enjoy for so many miserable years. With the power of life and death in his hands, read his response:

> Joseph said to his brothers, "Please come closer to me." And they came closer. And he said, "I am your brother Joseph, whom you sold into Egypt. Now do not be grieved or angry with yourselves, because you sold me here; for God sent me before you to preserve

life. For the famine has been in the land these two years, and there
are still five years in which there will be neither plowing nor har-
vesting. God sent me before you to preserve for you a remnant in
the earth, and to keep you alive by a great deliverance" (Genesis
45:4–7).

Now wait a minute, what gives? Did God actually send Joseph
before his brothers to save their lives, or did his brothers wickedly,
and with nothing but jealousy and malice, sell him into a living hell?
Which was it? Both!

I believe that for many years Joseph viewed his brothers' actions
from a very human perspective. It was only later, when God had
exalted him and used him to save many lives that he was able to see
from the rearview mirror of life what God had been doing. I don't
believe Joseph ever lost his faith, but it took a while before he gained
understanding and perspective.

There are going to be events that God uses, people He uses, pleasant experiences, and awful experiences that will combine in the divine
plan to move us directly into God's will for our lives. But, and this is
important, we won't be able to see any of this from our vantage point,
or understand it until years later. In some cases, we may never see it.

At times we simply won't know God's will. Deuteronomy 29:29
reminds us that "The secret things belong to the LORD our God, but
the things revealed belong to us and to our sons forever. . . ." He does
not treat us like mice in a maze, instantly rewarding us with food and
a flashing light for successfully running through all the obstacles.

This is where we learn, sometimes painfully, an important truth.
God wants us to trust in and depend upon His character, as revealed
through His Word, and not try to decipher His character from our
own experiences. Our short-term perspectives do not help us to draw
the correct conclusions from our miscellaneous circumstances. C. S.
Lewis once wrote, "No doubt all history in the last resort must be
held by Christians to be a story with a divine plot."[5] In some situations we may never conclusively know God's will for a certain circum-

stance. Either we don't have the time to see the change it will make in us, or we still lack the perspective to view it as God does. And we discover that this is one of God's great plans for our spiritual growth. Hebrews 11:6 reminds us that "without faith it is impossible to please Him, for he who comes to God must believe that He is, *and that He is a rewarder of those who seek Him*" (emphasis added).

Developing our atrophied muscles of faith is one of God's clear and undeniable goals. Seeking the will of God begins a journey of faith where we are constantly urged to grow closer and closer to Him in order to more clearly understand His plans and direction for us. The better you get to know someone, the more you come to understand his or her actions, character, and purposes.

At times we will need to retreat to Proverbs 3:5–6, "Trust in the Lord with all your heart *and do not lean on your own understanding*. In all your ways acknowledge Him, and He will make your paths straight" (emphasis added). We are left to trust, trust that our present difficult experiences are more than just the catastrophes that they seem to be; that our loss, or pain, was not designed to destroy us; that God is still good and loving, even when He allows bad and hurtful things to occur in our lives.

And time is often a necessary ingredient to arriving at this conclusion. What we have clung to by faith, in spite of circumstances, is often vindicated over time. As Paul said, there are things on this earth that we see dimly (1 Corinthians 13:12). Some things in life are just unclear and we can't always make sense out of them. God's will is often one of those things that we perceive very dimly.

So if you are too close to a painful experience, don't go crazy looking for all the answers. If you are in the midst of a trying time, don't worry that it doesn't all make sense to you right now. The clouds of pain and trouble are obscuring your view and your perspective.

You need time. I remember the first time I took off in a plane when it was overcast and rainy, and our plane gained enough altitude to rise above the storm. Suddenly we broke into sunshine and blue skies, and the clouds and rain and wind were all underneath us; I suddenly realized that the sun hadn't gone away, it was still exactly where it always had been. I had a perspective that few other people underneath those clouds could possibly have. What they knew only by faith, I now knew by experience. I could actually see and feel the warmth of the sun, where earlier I had felt only the cold and wet of the storm.

Like the sun, God never leaves, nor changes. He is as He has always been. His love is unchanging, His purposes are good and kind and beneficial, even when clouds of trouble seem to obscure that view of Him.

Be patient. Don't worry that you can't see everything right now, or understand everything right now. Just rest in the fact that God, like the sun, is there, and accomplishing His good purposes in our lives. It may take a while before you can say, "God has made me forget all my trouble," and there is no hurry. The storm will break, and the Son will shine through, and the view will be decidedly different.

Before we leave, let's take a look at one last thought about the will of God.

FOLLOW THROUGH

1. "We'll sometimes have to make decisions with precious little information, without knowing how those decisions will pan out." Have you ever experienced times like this?

2. Can the very struggle to discern God's will for your life *be* God's will for your life? How might this be true, and why?

3. Have you had an experience that caused you to feel you could echo Joseph's sentiments—"God has made me forget all my trou-

ble and all my father's household"? What happened—and how did God ease your pain in this area?

4. What do you think Joseph meant by the statement, "God has made me forget"? Does it mean he simply could not remember it, or do you think Joseph meant something else?

5. "At times we simply won't know God's will." What is the hardest part about this statement and its implications?

6. How can you be confident that God is doing good, even when you don't feel good?

Making Contact

When life is hard and we can't understand what God is doing, we need to cling to the testimony of Joseph and the faithfulness of God. Re-read Genesis 41:51–52, and trade places with Joseph. What is God doing with your life that you cannot understand at the moment? Then reread Genesis 45:4–7, and share a prayer of faith. "Lord, I don't know what You're doing, and life is very difficult to understand right now, but I will trust that You are leading me through this, not only for my sake, but for the sake of others also. Perhaps for my children, my spouse, my friends, or the lives of those I may never meet. Help me not to lose heart, nor seek all the answers to life. Simply strengthen my faith and trust in Your eternal loving character."

CHAPTER TWO

The Bush Won't Burn, And I'm All Out of Matches

He was forty years old, highly educated, and mingled freely with the ruling elite of society. Everyone knew his name. He was somebody to be reckoned with. But all his life he had lived with a secret, the knowledge that he was from a common people. He hadn't been born into this society, he had been plucked out, saved, delivered. Yes, that was the word, *delivered!*

That concept of deliverance began to grow in this man's heart. While he had been delivered from the toil and strain of everyday living, his people hadn't. So, with the idea of deliverance raging in his bosom, he visited his oppressed people.

As he surveyed the tragic scene, thousands of milling bodies, laboring under their taskmaster's cruel whips in the blazing sun, he witnessed a scene that threw him into a rage. One of his people was being unjustly abused by a taskmaster. A little man given a lot of power had let it go to his head. Confronting the abuser, the deliverer tried to even the score. But he let his emotions get the upper hand; he went too far. He killed the taskmaster. Quickly, he pulled the corpse into the bushes and left.

The next day he returned to his post, the post of the deliverer, guarding his charges. Spying two of his countrymen fighting with each other, he quickly attempted to break it up. Pulling them apart, he reminded them, "Why are you hitting your fellow Hebrew?" (Exodus 2:13 NIV). Another good deed done by the deliverer.

But before the patronizing smile had a chance to leave his face, he felt a jarring push. Who had dared to interfere? It was one of the two men who had been fighting, one of his fellow countrymen. "Who made you ruler and judge over us?" he snarled. "Are you thinking of killing me as you killed the Egyptian?" Undoubtedly, there was an evil look on his face that said, "I know, I saw, and I'm telling!" The ungrateful wretch!

The Egyptians would find out what the man had done, and who he really was, but perhaps most painful for the deliverer was the stunning realization that his countrymen didn't want him. Driven by fear and disappointment, he ran as far and as fast as he could. In a moment he had been transformed from the Who's Who of Egyptian social life, to self-appointed deliverer, to fugitive on the run. How quickly circumstances can change a life. He didn't stop running until he reached Midian. There he rescued some women from a group of rough and rowdy shepherds. (Old habits die hard.) From great deliverer to playing bodyguard to common shepherd girls. No longer the noble hero he had probably envisioned himself becoming; nevertheless, deliverance was still his passion.

As a reward he was given one of them as a wife, and then he became a shepherd himself. Gone were the expensive clothes, the exotic food, and the special treatment. Now it was he who was toiling with hard work and aching bones and rugged conditions. He would die as a common shepherd, unknown and obscure as any one of the thousands who still slaved in Egypt.

What was the purpose for it all? There wasn't any—couldn't be. Until one day, leading his sheep, he spies a bush on fire. He comes closer to investigate. If the fire grows, his sheep could be in danger. But, strangely, the fire doesn't spread; it just burns.

Moving close enough to see clearly, he is startled. The bush is burning, but all by itself. Nothing else, just the bush. And the bush isn't burning up, nothing is turning black, it's simply aflame. Walking nearer to it, he suddenly hears a voice coming from—it can't be—from the bush.

"Moses, Moses!" (Exodus 3:4). From here we know the story well. God speaks to Moses and introduces Himself from the burning bush. God has a plan for his life; Moses will be a deliverer after all. God talks with Moses, and gives him a blueprint for his life and the plan for Israel's rescue and exodus from Egypt.

We've heard that story, some of us, since we were little kids. Moses literally stumbles over the will of God. God plants Himself so flamboyantly in Moses' path that He can't be missed. He articulates His plan for Moses and the rest of his life so clearly that it can't be misunderstood. Furthermore, He does it face to face. Oh, for the good old days!

Moses never had to agonize over whether he was following God's will for his life. And while we love the story, at times we are tempted to call out, "Foul! That's not fair!"

Today, when we seek the will of God wholeheartedly, waiting for the tiniest bit of clear direction, we get no response. It seems that most of our lives we are walking around looking for that same burning bush. We never find it. Oh, we find bushes all right, and we do our best to duplicate Moses' experience. If our bush won't burn by itself, maybe we can light a fire underneath it. Maybe God will communicate His will to us too. Maybe He's waiting for us to take the first step.

So we agonize (one match).
And equivocate (one match).
And we pray (another match).
We read the Bible (another match).
We explain to God that this is an emergency (this is good for two matches at least).
We ask more "spiritual" people to set our bush on fire (another match).
We put out fleeces (a three-matcher if there ever was one).
We search our hearts carefully (another match).
We write "Dear Abby" (match breaks).

We read books, attend seminars, listen to tapes, until finally we realize—we're all out of matches!

The bush won't burn for us, and we're all out of matches! After all the things we've tried, all the spiritual calisthenics we've gone through, we often feel no closer to knowing God's will for our lives than we did before we started looking.

And it's not as if discovering God's will is simply an intellectual curiosity. It can mean the difference between the Promised Land and No Man's Land. When we want God to give us a simple true or false, yes or no, He seems to respond with multiple choice.

What is so frustrating is that the Bible states quite clearly that God seems intent on providing direction for each of us. Here are just a few of many verses relating to God's promised direction:

> I will instruct you and teach you in the way which you should go; I will counsel you with My eye upon you (Psalm 32:8).

> You guide me with your counsel, and afterward you will take me into glory (Psalm 73:24 NIV).

> Trust in the LORD with all your heart, and do not lean on your own understanding. In all your ways acknowledge Him, and He will make your paths straight (Proverbs 3:5–6).

> The LORD will guide you always (Isaiah 58:11 NIV).

> Do not be foolish, but understand what the will of the Lord is (Ephesians 5:17).

> Those who are led by the Spirit of God are sons of God (Romans 8:14 NIV).

Led? Who is being led? Common folks, just like you and me. How? That's what we need to know, isn't it?

We do not presume to know all there is about the will of God, for most of this information is kept by God, and He keeps His own counsel. Yet, we must look deeper, for God clearly desires to lead and guide us. Furthermore, the spiritual stakes are too high to leave this discussion to our impressions, feelings, or worse, scriptural ignorance. In fact, it is recognizing the inherent dangers of misunderstanding the will of God that prompted this work.

The importance of answering these questions can easily be seen by looking at a number of myths that arise from confusion concerning God's leading. I'd like to briefly address some of these, and then spend the next nine chapters dealing more completely with them, and others. We can begin with the following myth:

<u>MYTH #1</u>

God's Will Can Be Discovered Only by the Spiritual Elite

It is very tempting to conclude that God was able to lead Moses, and Elijah, and the other biblical Hall-of-Famers, but that's because they are in a different spiritual class than the rest of us. We think, *I haven't got the Bible memorized, don't have any seminary degrees, haven't rallied tens of thousands of believers, and don't pray five hours a day.* With this in mind it is easy to come to the conclusion that the clear leading of God seems to be available only for those who are "full-timers."

The only problem with that line of thinking is that what God told Moses, He told Moses to tell to the children of Israel. The lowest common laborer in Israel, in captivity to Egypt, heard the will of God. In fact, God made sure Moses told His people very clearly who He was, and what He wanted.

If we believe God's will for our lives cannot be known or actively pursued because we aren't among the spiritual elite, we won't seek it anymore. That's not the case. God is just as concerned with your knowing how to discern His leading as He is with Billy Graham's. His promises apply to all believers equally.

Another equally dangerous myth goes like this:

MYTH #2

You Have Misinterpreted the Will of God and It Can't Be Undone

Somewhere, sometime, you took a step you believed was in God's will. You were sure. Every signal was green. So you took the step, only to see it now end up in failure and disaster. It seems like everything has gone up in smoke.

You bought the home, took the job, started the business, accepted the responsibility, made the investment, had the baby, got the degree, only to see the bottom fall out. When this happens we can feel betrayed or misled by God. Still smarting from the pain of this experience, we're less than eager to seek God about direction again. What makes our pain deeper is that we really sought God's will with all our might, and yet we feel He didn't come through.

I remember talking with a deeply committed and godly Christian who had thrown himself into a certain ministry. It was an area of unquestionable promise, and he was sure that God's blessing was wrapped up in it. He sacrificed considerable time, energy, emotion, and even life savings, in the firm belief that God's will was being fulfilled—yet the ministry never materialized. Everything went up in smoke.

Deeply disappointed, he detailed his faithfulness to do all the things God would require for success. The look in his eyes was a mixture of hurt and disillusionment. It was apparent that he felt he had clearly kept up his end of the bargain, but God had somehow reneged.

Somehow he got his signals or God's signals crossed, and he was paying a horrible price for the mistake. What he did could not be undone. But why should he suffer for this mistake when he really did seek God's will? Why couldn't God cut him a little slack?

God's will, at times, seems very similar to the description Winston Churchill gave of Russia: "A riddle wrapped in a mystery inside an enigma."[6] Why should we be penalized for not being able to read God's mind?

The futility of our approach often leaves us shaking our heads in despair, until finally, we just give up. We certainly can't do any worse by ignoring Him, we decide. And eventually buried resentment and hurt feelings prompt us to slowly drift away from God, all over this issue of finding His will.

But is God's will like those annoying road signs hidden behind overgrown bushes or trees that we can so easily miss as we drive along in life? Can we so easily "oops" our way out of God's will?

This view would have God almost totally inattentive to our lives and not willing to intervene to help us—even when He knows we're trying to go the way He wants us to. In fact, in this view, God wouldn't really care if we found His will or not—an idea the Bible simply doesn't support.

I have seen people leave the ministry, leave the church, and tragically, even abandon their faith over issues like this. All because of a basic misunderstanding of discovering the will of God. And if this were not enough, here is another myth:

MYTH #3

The Will of God Always Involves a Supernatural Sign

The infamous Gideon's fleece (Judges 6–8). This is the idea that God must speak today as He spoke yesterday. Furthermore, nothing short of the miraculous or supernatural can lead to the discovery of God's will for our life. We can feel that we are to be passive observers while God pulls all the supernatural strings. So we read the story of Gideon in the Bible, about his unique way of determining God's will by putting out a wool fleece and asking God to miraculously give him a sign through it, and are convinced that is the divine formula for seeking God's will. This approach is a favorite of many, but often has led to tragic results.

A young man I knew years ago prayed for a job, and that is certainly the place to start, but unfortunately that was also the place he stopped. He would pray, at home, safely away from the car, the want ads, or any signs that said, "Help Wanted." He was expecting God to simply "bring" him a job. He felt it was a true test of faith and his spirituality. I suppose he's still waiting by the phone.

When we are convinced that a supernatural sign is really the divine formula for discovering God's will, it is easy to be misled by frivolous signs: We become superstitious sign-watchers.

"God, if you want me to tithe, then give me a 10 percent raise this year." (If He gives only 9 percent, does that mean I don't have to tithe?)

"Lord, if you want me to accept this man's proposal of marriage, let him call today between four and five o'clock."

"Lord, if you want me to take this job, then let the fourth car that I pass today be red."

Of course, if the sign doesn't come, we can feel we have been given an "excused from work" slip from heaven. In fact we can start to believe that if we don't get 100 percent divine confirmation in a dramatic way for some specific direction in life, we don't have to do anything at all. But we are going to see a number of people in Scripture who had to find God's will with no supernatural signs whatsoever.

Furthermore, Gideon's fleece experience is a superficially studied and occasionally misunderstood passage. Upon further investigation you will discover that Gideon didn't offer his fleece as a result of his great faith, but his *lack* of it. Gideon was asking for further signs to confirm the will of God *that had already been revealed to Him.*

Elisabeth Elliot, in *A Slow and Certain Light,* talks about the subject of guidance by the miraculous. She has this to say:

There is one thing we ought to notice about these miracles. When God guided by means of the pillar of cloud and fire, by the star of Bethlehem, by visitations of angels, by the word coming through visions and dreams and prophets and even through an insulted donkey, in most cases these were not signs that had been asked for. And when they were asked for, as in the case of Jehoshaphat and Ahab, they were not accepted.

Supernatural phenomena were given at the discretion of the divine wisdom. It is not for us to ask that God will guide us in some miraculous way. If, in his wisdom, he knows that such means are what we need, he will surely give them.[7]

This leads us to the next myth:

MYTH #4

God's Will Equals Smooth Sailing

This idea contends that because I'm experiencing great difficulties, I must be outside God's will or misreading God's leading. In other words, if I were in the perfect will of God for my life, I wouldn't face the problems and disasters I now encounter.

Unfortunately, the biblical evidence contradicts this conclusion. Daniel was in the perfect will of God for his life—in the lions' den. Joseph was in the perfect will of God for his life—in the pit, in slavery, and even prison. Paul was in the perfect will of God—in prison.

Peter and James and John were in the middle of God's will as they were being beaten and arrested for sharing Christ. And ultimately, Jesus, hanging on the cross, was in the perfect will of God!

We will examine this idea later. But now, another myth, becoming more prevalent in our Christian culture today goes something like this:

MYTH #5

Believers Should Rely on Emotions to Determine God's Will

"I felt God leading me to buy this business."

"I just felt God drawing me and this person at work together; I know it is of God. We both have a real peace about it. I know

God doesn't like divorce, but why else would He bring us together?"

"I felt God led me to give X amount of money to such and such a group, and now I don't have enough to pay the rent or buy food for my family. Oh well, He will provide for me."

I have heard all of these lines of reasoning, and more besides. With this line of thinking there are no clear parameters for discerning the leading of God, other than how we feel about something at the moment. And as we all know, our emotions can fluctuate wildly, reacting not only to reality, but also perceived reality. Thus, our feelings become to us the will of God, and ultimately we become gods unto ourselves. But are our emotions and feelings alone trustworthy enough to discover God's will? We will address this issue. But perhaps the greatest myth created by confusion about God's will is:

MYTH #6

When God Doesn't Act According to Our Expectations, Something Must Be Wrong with God

I once tried an enlightening exercise with a group of Christians, many of whom expressed frustration and confusion over the way God worked in their lives. Each of them had "sought the will of God" for something or other without any clear understanding of this important issue.

I simply asked them to draw a picture of how they perceived God looking at them, how they envisioned His expression toward them. The results would have depressed the most enthusiastic optimist.

When God didn't act in the way they expected Him to, they became suspicious of His intentions. When they expected Him to lead them into one kind of situation, believing that is what was promised them, and they found themselves in an entirely different set of circumstances, they began to believe that God is temperamental, distant, and unpredictable.

Some of us are terribly confused right now: on one hand we read and hear about a God who is loving, close, tender, forgiving, gracious, and eagerly watching over us and guiding us; yet on the other hand, because of our experiences with God, He seems more like an eccentric monarch, only vaguely aware of us, disinterested in letting us know what's on His mind, and angry when we're unable to decipher His wishes. We're not sure how to reconcile the God of the Bible with the God of our experiences.

If we do not come to a correct understanding of how God leads us, of how His will operates, and of how we are to follow His leading, we can develop a terribly distorted view of God that will keep us from coming to Him. It will keep us, in fact, afraid of Him. This is the greatest of all spiritual dangers.

We are going to cover all these myths and more, because finding God's will is a big deal to most of us. We've been told God has a perfect plan for our lives, but if we're honest, most of us would have to admit that we have no clue about how to discover what that is.

But before we close this chapter, we need to be reminded of some important truths. God loves you very much; He is acutely aware of and interested in your circumstances, your pain, your disasters. He knows you are confused about this, and He wants to bring understanding. Everything you read about God in Scripture is true, and while some of the truths you have read about Him seem to have gotten hopelessly tangled up with your experiences, God wants to untangle those truths for you.

God doesn't need burning bushes to lead His people, as we will see. So put away your matches, relax a little, listen a lot, search the Scriptures, and let's find out about the will of God together.

One of the first things to consider when we investigate God's will is something we've probably thought little about. It's called the relational imperative. Never heard of it? I'm not surprised. Let's take a look.

FOLLOW THROUGH

1. When I don't sense God answering my requests for direction, my response is usually to

2. The verse or passage or principle found in the Bible that I have always used to help guide my search for the will of God is

   (If you don't know the exact place, just paraphrase what you remember, and see if the group can find the exact location.)

3. The way I know that I have found the will of God is

4. What convinces one person that he or she has found the will of God in a particular instance, may not convince another. What does God have to do to convince me?

5. "I'm just not at a point in my spiritual life where I am mature enough to discern God's leading." Agree or disagree, and explain.

6. The last time I thought I knew God's will, but was mistaken, was

7. Reread Judges 6–8 for yourself. Why did Gideon set out his fleece in the first place? What kind of supernatural signs have I hoped God would use to direct me?

8. Choose either of these sentences and write a response to it:

   I believe I have discovered the will of God for my life right now because

   I believe I haven't found the will of God yet because

9. The last time I knew God's will for my life, despite the difficult circumstances I faced, was when

Making Contact

On a piece of paper, write your greatest questions concerning God's will for your life. Be as specific or as general as you want to be. Fold the paper and put it in a safe place where only you have access to it. Then, find a quiet place to speak to God. Ask God to take these questions and concerns and bring you greater understanding and insight as you work through this book. Commit yourself to prayer before reading each chapter, asking that God would use His Word to enlighten your heart.

When you find one of your questions answered in the process of reading this book, go back and put a line through that issue and privately thank God for His faithfulness to your prayers. Keep this with you until you have completed the book.

CHAPTER THREE

Who's on First?
Discovering the Relational Imperative

Have you ever been in a discussion with someone whose responses to your questions didn't make any sense at all? You can tell something is amiss when their answers seem not only inappropriate, but wacky.

Some of us may remember the golden days of radio, and the early days of TV. During this period the comic team of Abbott and Costello became household names and became legendary with their now-famous comedy skit, "Who's on First?" What follows is only the beginning of this skit, but you'll soon get the idea as Abbott and Costello try in vain to communicate with each other about the subject of baseball.

Costello begins the discussion:

Costello: "Well, you know I've never met the guys. So you'll have to tell me their names, and then I'll know who's playing on the team."

Abbott: "Oh, I'll tell you their names, but you know it seems to me they give these ball players nowadays very peculiar names."

Costello: "You mean funny names?"

Abbott: "Strange names, pet names . . . like Dizzy Dean. . . ."

Costello: "His brother Daffy."

Abbott: "Daffy Dean. . . ."

Costello: "And their French cousin."

Abbott: "French?"

Costello: "Goofè."

Abbott: "Goofè Dean. Well, let's see, we have on the bags, Who's on first, What's on second, I Don't Know is on third. . . ."

Costello: "That's what I want to find out."

Abbott: "I say, Who's on first, What's on second, I Don't Know's on third."

Costello: "Are you the manager?"

Abbott: "Yes."

Costello: "You gonna be the coach too?"

Abbott: "Yes."

Costello: "And you don't know the fellows' names?"

Abbott: "Well, I should."

Costello: "Well, then, who's on first?"

Abbott: "Yes."

Costello: "I mean the fellow's name."

Abbott: "Who."

Costello: "The guy on first."

Abbott: "Who."

Costello: "The first baseman."

Abbott: "Who."

Costello: "The guy playing. . . ."

Abbott: "Who is on first!"

Costello: "I'm asking YOU who's on first."

Abbott: "That's the man's name."

Costello: "That's who's name?"

Abbott: "Yes."

Costello: "Well, go ahead and tell me."

Abbott: "That's it."

Costello: "That's who?"

Abbott: "Yes."

"Who's on First?" is as funny now as it was when it was originally recorded by Abbott and Costello. In this hilarious discussion, Costello asks Abbott about the names of the players on a particular baseball team.

Unknown to Costello, all the players on the team have silly names, like "Who," "What," and "I Don't Know." It is funny from our point of view because we can see that while Abbott is very honestly and carefully answering all of Costello's questions, the answers don't make any sense to Abbott. The more he asks, the more the answers confuse him, and with each answer he doesn't understand, his confusion and frustration grow.

At times, isn't this how we feel when we ask God for direction? We can't help wondering if, during our discussions with God, an angelic audience isn't watching the whole thing and rolling in the aisles. It is funny when it's Abbott and Costello, but not so amusing when it is God and us.

While God would never deceive us, or deliberately attempt to communicate in a way we couldn't understand, there are times when His answers to our requests for direction seem so strange that we wonder if He hasn't gotten us mixed up with Harry or Mary in Duluth.

I've felt that way—more than once. And it took me years to finally understand what was going on. All my notions about why God was so confusing were mistaken. Why wasn't I hearing God right? Why wasn't I receiving the directions I was sincerely seeking?

GOING OUT OF RANGE

For years my family and I would drive north for vacation, a significant trip that took us hundreds of miles away from home. We always began this long journey very early in the morning, when all the kids were asleep and my wife and I were a little groggy. To keep us awake, we turned to our favorite radio station and listened to music. For a while everything was fine, but after an hour or two on the road, the station began to fade, and our favorite songs were interrupted by static. As we journeyed into the mountains, the station eventually faded out completely and was replaced by silence.

What happened? Well, of course, nothing complicated. Our radio is a receiver that picks up signals sent by the radio stations and the signals from our local stations can travel only a limited distance. The further out we went, the weaker the signals became, and the fuzzier our reception. The station's signals were strong as ever, but we had moved out of range. There was nothing wrong with the signals; the problem was with the receiver. The longer we drove, the further out of range we took ourselves.

The same is true with God's will and us. When, after repeated attempts to receive a signal from God, we get only fuzzy reception, or mere silence, we often assume that the problem is with the sender.

But rest assured, this is not a new problem. Let's look at Deuteronomy 29:2–4.

> Moses summoned all Israel and said to them, "You have seen all that the LORD did before your eyes in the land of Egypt to Pharaoh and all his servants and all his land; the great trials which your eyes have seen, those great signs and wonders. Yet to this day the LORD has not given you a heart to know, nor eyes to see, nor ears to hear."

Now here, Moses is talking to the very people who had been led out of Egypt by signs and wonders. They were the same folks who had gotten miraculous, supernatural, abundantly clear directions on exactly what God wanted them to do and exactly where He wanted them to go. A cloud by day, and a fire by night. These are the people we envy, because they had what we don't.

Yet, in spite of the unmistakably clear and supernatural direction they had been given, their greatest problem was they didn't have eyes to see, or ears to hear. How could one become hard of hearing with that kind of divine activity going on?

But did you hear what God said? He said, in effect, "You saw, but you can't see. You heard Me, but you can't hear." Clearly there is more to discerning the will of God for our lives than just receiving precise road map directions.

In Isaiah chapter 59, the prophet laments the same condition with the people of his day, hundreds of years later. In Isaiah 59:1–4, 7–10 we read:

> Behold, the LORD's hand is not so short that it cannot save; nor is His ear so dull that it cannot hear. But your iniquities have made a separation between you and your God, and your sins have hidden His face from you so that He does not hear. For your hands are defiled with blood and your fingers with iniquity; your lips have spoken falsehood, your tongue mutters wickedness. No one sues righteously and no one pleads honestly. They trust in confusion and speak lies; they conceive mischief and bring forth iniquity. . . . Their feet run to evil, and they hasten to shed innocent blood; their thoughts are thoughts of iniquity; devastation and destruction are in their highways. They do not know the way of peace, and there is no justice in their tracks; they have made their paths crooked; whoever treads on them does not know peace.
>
> Therefore, justice is far from us, and righteousness does not overtake us; *we hope for light, but behold, darkness; for brightness, but we walk in gloom. We grope along the wall like blind men, we grope like those who have no eyes; we stumble at midday as in the twilight, among those who are vigorous we are like dead men* (emphasis added).

Get the picture in the last verse. Here are people, just like us, groping around, blindly. "We hope for light, but behold, darkness; for brightness, but we walk in gloom." What a picture of where we often are when trying to find God's will. What was the problem? The same one mentioned in Psalm 66:18: "If I regard wickedness in my heart, the Lord will not hear."

Many years later, Jesus spoke of this problem too. In Matthew 13:15, He quotes Isaiah, saying, "THE HEART OF THIS PEOPLE HAS BECOME DULL, WITH THEIR EARS THEY SCARCELY HEAR, AND THEY HAVE CLOSED THEIR EYES, OTHERWISE THEY WOULD SEE WITH THEIR EYES, AND HEAR WITH THEIR EARS, AND UNDERSTAND WITH THEIR HEART AND RETURN, AND I WOULD HEAL THEM."

Again, notice, there is a distinct problem with hearing and seeing the truth of God that is right under their noses. And this twitch of human nature hasn't disappeared; it's alive and well. You have it and I have it.

What these verses tell us is that we have a tendency to miss something absolutely essential about God. And this something we're missing comes directly into play when we seek God's will for our lives and come up empty.

We can learn from these passages some truths that can revolutionize our thinking on this issue. The first thing we will see is that:

Knowing the Will of God Begins with the Person of God

While sin was the issue, it doesn't explain the whole problem. Isaiah recorded for us the legacy of a people who wanted the leading of God, but didn't want to walk with God. In other words, they wanted a talisman God, a Ouiji-board God, who would reveal to them the mysteries of the future, and give them good advice. But, they had no interest in God Himself, in His holiness, His righteousness, His justice. They just wanted a genie who would do their bidding.

So when God didn't give them what they were after, they accused Him of not being able to hear them, or of being unable to provide for them. God assured them that His arm wasn't too short to deliver them, and He wasn't hard of hearing. His message was clear, but their receivers were plugged. Furthermore, they probably would have been surprised to discover what God's message was.

The will of God is intricately connected with the person of God. Therefore, establishing and maintaining the relationship with Him takes priority over gaining direction from Him. Because maintaining the relationship *is* His direction. When we are trying to get on with bigger and better things, and feel that God is dragging His feet, it is often because His priority beyond everything else is our relationship with Him.

Because God is a person, He leads relationally, one personal being leading another personal being. This relationship is essential for communication to be effective. And when a relationship has been strained or broken by apathy, or infidelity, the lines of communication are impaired. We are God's children; He is a tender Father, caring and deeply concerned for our welfare.

When we sin, we don't just break a law, we offend God because His law is a reflection of His person, His eternal character. To break His law, therefore, is to personally offend Him. Before any further progress can be made, and further direction given, the breach in the relationship needs to be repaired. This truth is expressed in the following:

(Since) Sin halts relational progress.
(And) Relational repair is essential for further direction.
(Therefore) Sin halts directional progress.

The priority needs to be repairing and cultivating the relationship. One of the reasons we have such a problem with this today is that we get confused about the popular Christian buzz-phrase, "personal relationship." We tell those who don't yet know Christ as their Savior that they need a personal relationship with God. And that's true. But we don't often understand the extent to which that must be true—in our own lives. Many of us who claim to have a personal relationship with Christ have a relationship only in the legal sense.

LEGAL VERSUS INTIMATE

A personal relationship with Christ has two aspects to it. The legal, and the intimate, or personal. The legal aspect is where God takes us and makes us His spiritual children in a legal adoption; God commits Himself to us legally. We are no longer spiritual orphans, but become His precious children. He gives us a new home in heaven. We receive forgiveness, peace with God, and an eternal inheritance; God treats us differently than He did before. That is the legal aspect of the adoption, and certainly that is all wonderful news. But there is more to the relationship than just those legal realities.

Let me illustrate from my own experience. I was adopted at the age of twelve by one Dr. Schaeffer. He and my mother had decided to marry, and he wanted to adopt her three children. That might sound noble, but the real reason he wanted to adopt us was that he didn't want children in his family who didn't have his last name; he felt it would be embarrassing when he introduced us. In truth, we were adopted before he really even knew us—or could form any kind of emotional attachments. So this was not an intimate gesture on his part. But legally, I gained a whole new position in the world. He took on the responsibility for my care, provision, shelter, and schooling. I became an heir, got a new name, and several other positive advantages. I never lacked for food, clothing, shelter, or even many of the finer things of life.

I entered into a legal relationship with him, but there was nothing personal or intimate about it. We were friendly and civil, but that was about it. It never went any further, because he never pursued it any further.

Sometimes as Christians we do the same thing with God. We enter into a legal relationship and become His children: we are on decent terms with Him most of the time, and we are civil and friendly, but that is about it.

While I can honestly say that I didn't hate Dr. Schaeffer, I didn't really love him either; I was basically indifferent. And for both myself and Dr. Schaeffer that was fine. But God isn't Dr. Schaeffer, and that kind of relationship isn't enough. Because God is our creator, He wants us to cry out to Him, "Abba, Father," literally "Daddy." Because He is love, He seeks an intimate relationship with us, and He will continue to seek that depth of relationship regardless of how we respond.

To us the legal relationship with God may be enough, and we may stop with that. That may even make it easier when we sin against Him—we won't feel so bad. But it isn't enough to God.

During those times when we can't seem to get any clear direction from God, we start pointing frantically in all different directions and saying, "God, which way do I go?" He then answers, "This way!" and points to Himself. And we say, "No, you don't understand, God. I've got choices to make, decisions to finalize; now if You want to get in on these, You'd better speak up." Then we start pointing our hands in different directions again. And again He says, "I understand perfectly, You need to come this way," and He motions us toward Himself. We don't get it, do we? We've ignored the relational imperative.

DEFIANT AND DEMANDING

Have you ever seen defiant, rebellious children interact with their parents? Intimacy is completely absent, and they are indifferent to the pain this causes their parents. But this won't keep them from begging for their allowances, or special privileges. It seems the worse they treat their parents, the more they will demand from them.

I vividly remember a boy we'll call Billy (not his real name) in the town where I grew up. Billy's parents were wonderful people, but unable or unwilling to discipline little Billy. Billy was a holy terror! They were an affluent couple, and therefore able to give little Billy whatever he wanted, and Billy wanted plenty! But the more they gave little Billy presents to quiet his tantrums, and to get him to do what they wanted, the more wretchedly he treated them.

Defiant children treat their parents like incompetent clerks, with whose service they are totally dissatisfied. A parent cannot give effective direction to such a child because that child isn't interested in following anyone's directions but his own. They are seeking different ends. They aren't on the same page. All progress in the relationship between the child and parent stops, and only relationship repair will start it again.

When we stop respecting the personal relationship God wants to have with us, and become defiant, or rebellious, or worse, indifferent to Him, we have ignored the relational imperative. And yet, ironically, like defiant children, it seems that this is the time when we are most demanding of God, most apt to treat Him as some incompetent clerk who failed to understand our simple requests, or didn't deliver to us what we clearly ordered.

It has been my experience that the further we are from God relationally, because sin has moved us out of range of His will, the more we will demand of Him, and expect from Him.

But God isn't a cosmic tour guide, or a crystal ball that we can use for direction regardless of whether or not we're on good terms. He is our Father, our "Daddy." He leads us, not because He owes us something, or because we've paid for the service, but because He loves us so very deeply. He is motivated by a love relationship. He loved us to death, literally!

When our children are being disciplined at home, it doesn't do them any good to talk about an upcoming trip or activity. Until the relationship between us is healed by a changed attitude and action, all future plans go on the back burner. They're sent to their rooms, and the intimacy of the relationship grinds to a halt. Our expressions change, even though deep love still flows from parent to child.

They never stop being our children, and we never for a moment stop loving them. Our legal relationship will never be altered, but intimacy and fellowship are injured by sin and the future is no longer an issue. What is imperative at the moment is restoring our relationship. They hurt the relationship because of sin, and they need to take the necessary steps to restore it.

Some of us may be struggling with the issue of why God doesn't seem to be giving us any clear direction. Could it be that all the time you thought God wasn't hearing you, wasn't responding to you, He really was, but you were out of range? Maybe God was beckoning you to something that at the time you couldn't fully comprehend, something deeper, an intimate relationship with Him. Expecting a different answer, you didn't quite know what to do with what God was saying.

When we talk about discovering the will of God, we must address the issue of the relational imperative.

ACCEPTING THE RELATIONAL IMPERATIVE

As hard as it may seem at the moment, with large foreboding decisions looming over us for which we desperately want direction, we need to deal with the priority of our heavenly Father. He will not be swayed from His course by any tantrums from us.

Whatever our condition, whether we still feel close to God, or He seems a million miles away, we must begin to address this issue in our lives.

This isn't as easy as it sounds, and I don't want to make it seem too simplistic, for some of us have never experienced intimacy with anyone. We keep everyone at arm's length. We're not trying to be distant with God, but we've simply treated Him like everyone else in our life. Someone once wisely said that when we become a Christian, God begins the process of reparenting us.

For myself, I needed to make a conscious distinction between God and my human parents. God is not Mom or Dad; He is God. He does not fail, does not leave, does not berate, and He does not ever give up on me. His smile is ever on His face as He speaks with me, and His gentle hand is always on my shoulder to guide me. He knows me better than I know myself. Furthermore, and this is important, He knows what I'm afraid of—even at times when my fear is getting too close to Him.

I am convinced that one of the reasons so many people are clamoring to the offices of counselors these days is that they long to have a deeper relationship with someone—and are unable. They want intimacy, they sense that is the source of their emptiness, but they are also afraid of it. But we often are afraid of intimacy because we fear how people will react when they discover the "real" me. Maybe they won't like me. But God already knows the real you. He not only knows all your good points, He knows your bad ones too. He is intimately acquainted with you. And we have the benefit of knowing how He will react to us.

> God, being rich in mercy, because of His great love with which He loved us, even when we were dead in our transgressions, made us alive together with Christ (by grace you have been saved), and raised us up with Him, and seated us with Him in the heavenly places in Christ Jesus (Ephesians 2:4–6).

Did you ever really understand that your heavenly Father is "rich in mercy"? Mercy is withholding punishment that is rightly deserved.

Sometimes we keep aloof from God out of fear that we have taxed God's mercy to the breaking point, and He will finally say, "Enough!" But that's precisely why Paul reminds us that He is "rich" in mercy.

Bill Gates is certainly one of the world's richest men. It would probably amuse Bill Gates if he had a son who one day came up to him meekly, with a trembling voice and asked, "Please, Dad, do you have ... could you possibly spare ... is there any way you could see yourself clear to give me a ... a ... dime?"

As silly as that picture is to us, that's how silly we look when we hope and pray for God to be merciful to us, His own children. He is not stingy in mercy, He is rich in mercy, and if you are His child, then you are His heir. Can you come nearer the God of all mercy when He calls to you? Can you take that giant step from the legal into the intimate?

Now this isn't something you can just jump into, but you can make a start. We can pray the most feeble words that we are sure don't come close to doing justice to what we feel or God wants, but if they are sincere, those prayers can move mountains—or even us! You can say, "God, I never fully understood how You wanted to have an intimate relationship with me. I realize that I have been unwittingly treating You like a tour guide, or a clerk, keeping You at arm's length. But I know now that You want me to be closer to You. Help me to treat You more like a person in my prayers and my thoughts. Help me to see the personal words You use in the Bible when You speak to me. Help me to see Your heart, God. Help me to lose my fear of intimacy with You. Help me to experience an intimacy with You that I could never have with anyone else."

Knowing the will of God begins with a personal relationship to God. The second truth takes this relationship a step further.

Knowing the Will of God Continues by Addressing the Issue of Sin

God can be offended and jealous of our straying from Him. He wants us back—but not just to re-submit our orders. The offense must be dealt with on our end.

God never stops talking with us, but sin can take us out of range of His voice. Remember the words of Isaiah, "Your iniquities [sins] have made a separation between you and your God" (59:2).

Separation! Now that's a word we understand in our culture, isn't it? It is an ugly word conveying a still uglier picture. If someone were to ask us how our relationship with God was going, we'd probably never think to use that term, but often it would be accurate. "So, Betty, how's your relationship with God going?" "Well, Sue, we're separated right now." "We're separated." Isn't that a tragic description of our relationship with God?

Now the Bible teaches clearly that nothing can separate us from the love of God, or our eternal relationship with Him—God will never divorce His bride, nor will He ever separate from us (Romans 8:35)! Hallelujah! Our eternal relationship with Him is forever secure. But sin does separate us from Him—it disturbs the closeness of our relationship. God's will for our future is placed in the background for the moment, shoved aside by the urgency of the relationship repair. In these moments the will of God isn't "Yes" or "No," this way or that way, buy or rent, take the job or turn it down; it is reconciliation.

Remember, the conquest of the Promised Land ground to a screeching halt because of unconfessed sin. Because Christ paid for all our sins, if we have trusted Him for our salvation, our legal relationship with God can never be broken, ever. But our intimacy can.

God's will is intimately connected with the person of God; therefore repairing our relationship will take priority over direction. All those times I wanted to change the subject and move on to bigger and better things, God said, "No, start here. Start with Me. Get right with Me first, then all the other things will fall in place." Jesus reminded us to "seek first His kingdom and His righteousness, and all these things will be added to you" (Matthew 6:33).

Both accepting the relational imperative and addressing sin are not quick steps that we can set down in a few minutes and walk through. It is a reflective process that we will be fine-tuning throughout our life. It is part and parcel of walking in the light.

Too often we picture our Christianity as membership in a warehouse store, where wonderful goodies and treasures, previously unavailable to us, are now within our reach. To hear some preachers talk you'd think that was the case.

But we were adopted into a family, betrothed to an eternally loving and faithful groom. Upon salvation we entered first and foremost a relationship with a relational God. He wants to lead us relationally. Whatever questions we may have concerning the leading of God in our lives must begin with that glorious truth.

Now, I know what some of you are thinking. *That's good stuff, Dan. Now, about finding the will of God for my life!*

No, I haven't gotten off the subject, I just wanted to start out right. But rest assured, God offers definite guidelines that help us understand His will.

FOLLOW THROUGH

1. If I had to pinpoint my present relationship with God on a line I would place it: (Make an X anywhere on the line.)

   Legal . . . . Intimate

   Explain why you placed your X where you did.

2. Being as honest as possible, explain what you think is keeping you from being more intimate in your relationship with God.

3. How much can you identify with the defiant and demanding child named Billy in your relationship with God?

4. It was stated in this chapter that "the further away we are from God relationally, because sin has moved us out of range of His will, the more we will demand of Him, and expect of Him." How much do I identify with this statement?

5. I'm not trying to be distant with God, but I think what sometimes holds me back is

6. Reread Ephesians 2:4–6, slowly. Stop and think about the phrase, "But God, being rich in mercy. . . ." On a piece of paper, write down anything that I'm involved in that I sense might tax the mercy of

God toward me. Now finish the sentence: "God, knowing You are rich in mercy, I confess to You the following things.

7. Circle the word that you feel best describes your relationship with God at the present. Explain why.

cordial	intimate	suspicious
civil	distant	apprehensive
friendly	aloof	gun-shy
separated	cold	

8. Write out Romans 8:35 on a piece of paper this way: "Who will separate me from the love of Christ? Will. . . . ?" When you get to the word *will*, enter your own list of items that you may be tempted to think can separate you from God. Then go on to write, "For I am convinced that neither [enter again your own list of items] will be able to separate me from the love of God."

Making Contact

Intimacy with God begins with God, not with others. When we realize we can tell God everything, confess anything, admit anything, and He will still love and accept us, we begin the process of building (or re-building) intimacy. From there we can begin to slowly allow others into our circle of intimacy. But we will never be able to tell others, even loved ones, the things we can feel free to tell God. Our greatest opportunity for intimacy is with God first, people second.

If you've erected any barrier to keep God relationally distant, take a few moments in prayer and begin to speak to God the way you would to another person. If you've offended Him, apologize. If you are involved in a sin that you are sure is causing distance relationally, confess it to Him, and be specific. Then ask for His help in resisting this sin in the future. Don't worry about how to sit, or hold your hands; it is your heart that God is concerned with. Be honest and transparent.

CHAPTER FOUR

You Can't Get There from Here

I'll go where You want me to go, dear Lord,
O'er mountain, or plain, or sea;
I'll say what You want me to say, dear Lord,
I'll be what You want me to be.

—Mary Elizabeth Brown[8]

This poem expresses what so many other poems, songs, and sermons have said at one time or another. It is a beautiful and laudable sentiment. "Lord, whatever you want me to do, I'll do it!" The only problem we can see is that He just doesn't get around to telling us what He wants us to do!

Or, does He?

One of the questions that I have heard most often in my years as a pastor goes something like this: "What does God want me to do; what is His will for my life? I'm willing to do whatever He wants me to do, if He'd just tell me."

I remember hearing a young man asking me that some years back. And I remember answering him, "You know what He wants you to do." He looked at me quizzically, and said, "No, I don't."

"Yes, you do."

"No, I don't," he said growing slightly impatient with me. Then I calmed him down by saying, "Does God want you to study His Word?"

"Well, yes."

"Does God want you to attend church?"

"Certainly!"

So I continued to ask him a number of obvious questions concerning God's will. Then I said, "Well, it looks to me like you do know God's will." A funny look came over his face. He smiled and said, "Yeah, I guess I do."

"So, how are you doing with what you know?"

Clearly, what this young man was trying to get at was what was the concealed will of God for his life? Where did God want him to go to college, whom did He want him to marry, where did He want him to live? What was his special life purpose? These are the hidden things of God's will, the secret things, and these are of the utmost interest. My friend was one of those people who all too casually say, "I'm willing to do whatever God wants me to do, if He'd only *show* me what it is."

After listing a number of the things revealed by God about His will, it became apparent to him that he wasn't doing even those things. So by his own example he was proving that he wasn't really willing to do whatever God wanted him to do, if He'd only tell him.

We have a desire to be led by the supernatural, the burning bush, the cloud by day and fire by night. We want to know what's around the next corner, because we don't like surprises. At some point in your life you might have thought to yourself, *If only God would tell me what He wants me to do, I'd do it!*

Many of us have developed the idea that God is more interested in hiding His will for us than revealing it to us. Yet, the Bible clearly teaches the opposite.

> For this reason also, since the day we heard of it, we have not ceased to pray for you and to ask that you may be filled with the knowledge of His will in all spiritual wisdom and understanding, so that you will walk in a manner worthy of the Lord, to please Him in all respects, bearing fruit in every good work and increasing in the knowledge of God (Colossians 1:9–10).

Now, does that sound like God is interested in keeping His will from us? God wants us to be "filled" with the knowledge of His will.

The trouble is, we are often looking for specific information, "secret" information that we are sure we need in order to make the decisions we need to make. The Bible may have some interesting information in it, you may say, but it doesn't tell me whether I should attend USC or UCLA, marry Linda or Sally, or take this job or that one. These are the things that capture our attention. We don't question the known, we're interested in the unknown. It is interesting to note that Colossians was written to counter the Gnostic heresy that there was some kind of "secret knowledge" that only the spiritually elite had.

Further in the book of Colossians, Paul says, "Epaphras, who is one of your number, a bondslave of Jesus Christ, sends you his greetings, always laboring earnestly for you in his prayers, that you may stand perfect and fully assured in all the will of God" (4:12).

This verse, and many others, clearly show that God is not on a campaign to keep information from us. But it does seem that His method for delivering that information is different from what we expect. We want God to release the "secret" information, while He often leads an entirely different way. We want to step out by discovering the "unrevealed" information, while God wants us to put the right foot forward, by stepping out in obedience to His revealed will.

"The Holy Spirit expects us to take seriously the answers He has already provided, the light He has already shed," writes Paul Little, "and He does not expect us to plead for things that have already been denied."[9]

God said as much in Proverbs 3:5–6, where we read, "Trust in the Lord with all your heart, and do not lean on your own understanding. *In all your ways acknowledge Him, and He will make your paths straight*" (emphasis added).

What part does the revealed will of God play in leading us directly into the concealed will of God for our lives? How many times have we been on our way to someplace we are sure we know how to get to, and all of a sudden look around and realize that nothing looks familiar?

Coming home from Auburn, California, one year, we had to pass through Sacramento, and a tricky freeway interchange. It's easy to take a wrong turn. I'd asked for directions before I left just to make sure I'd remember, but instead of looking at the directions, I trusted my instincts. My wife, who is normally my navigator, had put her seat back to get some rest.

About an hour into the drive, having already passed through Sacramento, I looked out the window of the van and noticed some disturbingly unfamiliar scenery. I casually asked Annette, "Honey, what do those look like to you over there?" She glanced up for a moment and said, "They look like rice fields," then sat back again.

"Rice fields, really?"

"Yes, those are rice fields."

"Wow, I've never seen rice fields before."

"You have now."

Then, after a pause designed to put her off the scent, I asked nonchalantly, "Say, Annette, have you ever seen rice fields on the way home from Sacramento?"

Suddenly Annette bolted up and looked around quickly. In an instant she grasped the situation. "You took the wrong turn, we're on the wrong freeway, we're headed for San Francisco."

"Rice fields, so that's what rice fields look like."

"I can't believe you took the wrong turn."

"Honey, do you see any off-ramps anywhere?"

"None! I can't believe you took the wrong turn. Didn't you follow the directions?"

Eventually we did find an off-ramp, and we had to go all the way back to where I had taken the wrong turn. We lost valuable time, and all the while I was musing about how interesting those rice fields were Annette kept mumbling, "I can't believe you took the wrong turn."

As we seek to put the right foot forward in discussing God's will, there are some principles we can use to guide us.

Learn to Trust Your Directions Instead of Your Instincts

The next time I took that freeway, I was extremely attentive to the directions and the signs. I didn't trust my instincts. The junction where I made a wrong turn had several options that looked very similar. In fact, each option was separated by only a few feet; the width of one car lane. Yet, while the right road and wrong road were so close to each other there, the wrong turn eventually took me many miles away from my destination. When I followed my directions, my path was made straight. I again knew that I was heading in the right direction. David in Psalm 37:23 says, "The steps of a man are established by the LORD, and He delights in his way." In verse 31 he continues, "The law of his God is in his heart; his steps do not slip." What keeps him from misstepping? The directions he already has! God's Word puts us in the right lane in life. It takes an intentional detour from our direction to get back off the royal highway. Pastor and author Erwin Lutzer said it this way: "Obedience to revealed truth guarantees guidance in matters unrevealed."[10]

Admit That You Can't Get There from Here

When I get lost, I usually don't try to go back to where I took a wrong turn and correct it; I try to find some way to "get there from here." I don't want to go back and undo my wrong turn, take the right turn instead of the left. That's too much work, and I prefer shortcuts. And with freeways, it is sometimes possible to take shortcuts; with God's will, it is not.

There is a fascinating story in the book of Joshua, where Joshua is leading the people of Israel into the Promised Land. They had just conquered the mighty city of Jericho with its formidable defenses and mighty men; however, God had placed a ban on the items in Jericho. They were not to take any of them for themselves. Unknown to Joshua, though, one man, Achan, took some of the things that were banned. The next battle the Hebrews had was to take Ai, and it was reported to be a little insignificant area. In fact they were counseled not to take the whole army, just a few thousand could do the job. So they went—and got routed by little Ai. Now this wasn't just a case of the little train who thought he could make it over the great big hill, but something far more serious, as we're going to see. But poor Joshua couldn't understand it.

> Joshua said, "Alas, O Lord God, why did You ever bring this people over the Jordan, only to deliver us into the hand of the Amorites, to destroy us? If only we had been willing to dwell beyond the Jordan! O Lord, what can I say since Israel has turned their back before their enemies? For the Canaanites and all the inhabitants of the land will hear of it, and they will surround us and cut off our name from the earth. And what will You do for Your great name?" So the Lord said to Joshua, "Rise up! Why is it that you have fallen on your face?" (Joshua 7:7–10).

While Joshua was busy moaning about how terrible this defeat looked, and the disastrous impact it would have on their enemies' morale, God said, "Joshua, there is only one reason why you would not be given victory, victory that I have promised to give to you. Don't act surprised. Sin is the culprit." God expected Joshua to know precisely why they had been defeated: Someone ignored the directions.

Maybe Achan had a habit of stealing, or he may have thought that with all the people fighting and running around, no one would notice his one little disobedience. But that one little disobedience did matter. In fact, in verse 12 we read God's response: "I will not be with you anymore unless you destroy the things under the ban from your midst."

We can come to church every Sunday, lead Bible studies, worship like angels, and be involved in every good work that comes down the pike. But if we have ignored God's directions in some area of life, and trusted our own instincts, we are removing ourselves from the path of His will for us. We can't get there from here!

"A glimpse of the next three feet of road is more important and useful than a view of the horizon," wrote C. S. Lewis.[11]

REREADING THE DIRECTIONS

Interestingly, when the sin was uncovered, confessed, and dealt with, God gave Ai into their hands easily. Then we read of Joshua doing a very interesting and noteworthy thing.

> Afterward he read all the words of the law, the blessing and the curse, according to all that is written in the book of the law. There was not a word of all that Moses had commanded which Joshua did not read before all the assembly of Israel with the women and the little ones and the strangers who were living among them (Joshua 8:34–35).

They went back and reread the directions, so it wouldn't happen again! That's the problem with our instincts. We think we can take a wrong turn and it won't matter because I can get there from here. So, our instincts say, "There's got to be a shortcut." A shortcut to respect, maturity, success, love, and acceptance. So we put the directions somewhere out of sight, and head out. Our instincts say, "I can get there from here. I can disregard this one little direction and it won't make any difference in the scheme of God's will for me. I'll still end up where God wants me." Some have said:

> "I may not be loving my spouse, but I think I am still in the will of God. One wrong turn won't matter. I can get to His perfect will for my life from here."

> "I may not be keeping my word, but I think God will still guide me in His perfect will. I can get there from here."

> "I may not be reading the Bible, but my instincts are pretty good, because I'm a decent person. God will still be able to lead me where He wants me to go. I can get there from here."

"I have tried to follow God's instructions, except for this one area, but I'm mostly in His will. That's close enough. I can get there from here."

They should have put that on Achan's tombstone: "He thought he could get there from here." But after we've admitted that we can't get there from here, the next principle to putting the right foot forward is

---

Be Willing to Retrace Your Steps

Ironically, it is often true that we are most interested in God's concealed will when we are patently ignoring His revealed will. But to discover God's perfect will for our lives from that place is impossible; we must retrace our steps.

And after the first wrong turn, each ensuing wrong turn is all the easier to make. Each time we fail to "acknowledge Him in all our ways," we go a little further down the wrong road.

We once lived about thirty minutes from Disneyland. Let's say someone offered us directions to find that park. The instructions were clear and simple: get on the 5 freeway heading north, until I get to the Katella off-ramp. From there I should simply follow the signs to the Disneyland parking lot. Easy enough.

Those are the clear directions I receive. But I don't like traveling the 5; it is narrow, and bumpy, and dangerous at points, and the scenery isn't much to look at. So instead of taking the 5 north, I decide to take the 405 north. It heads in the same general direction, north, and is a much nicer drive, and a better freeway. Now I promise to obey *all* the other directions, just this one little change. It won't make much of a difference anyway. The only problem is that after 30 minutes, I don't see the Katella off-ramp anywhere and Disneyland is nowhere in sight. "Hey Annette, does anything around here look like Disneyland?"

Until I retrace my steps and realize where I started to go wrong, I am going to continue to go in circles, and get mad at whoever gave me these lousy directions. It is amazing how mad people can get at God for having given them such lousy directions. They simply can't see how ignoring simple directions had much of an impact on the fact that they are lost and vulnerable and in dangerous territory. They want to change Proverbs 3:6 to read, "In *a few* of my ways I acknowledged Him, and therefore He *ought* to have made my paths straight." The problem is they are leading with the wrong foot. You can't get there from here!

LETTING GOD DEAL WITH THE OBSTACLES

A more careful reading of the Hebrew word in Proverbs 3:6, indicates that "mak[ing] your paths straight" means more than just guidance. It literally means that God will remove the obstacles and smooth the way before us.

Several years ago, when the Northridge earthquake hit southern California, it toppled several freeways and created obstacles. Formidable ones. Passage on those roads was impossible for several months, but when I traveled north a while after the quake, I was detoured smoothly around that freeway, because someone else had dealt with the obstacles. I didn't have to go out by myself and try to move those incredible pieces of concrete out of the way and make a smooth path for my car. It would have been impossible.

Yet, we often try to do that in our lives. We come across an obstacle to trusting in the Lord with all our hearts, and in all our ways acknowledging Him. Inevitably something will pop up and try to convince us that continuing on this road is impossible.

So we spend a great deal of spiritual energy explaining to God why we need to take a left where He clearly tells us to make a right. What we point to are the obstacles in the way of our obedience to His will.

"But, Lord, if I do what You tell me to do, I'll lose money."
"Do what I say anyway, and I'll deal with that obstacle."
"But, Lord, if I do what You say, I might lose that friendship."
"Do what I say anyway, and I'll deal with that obstacle."

"But, Lord, if I do what You say, I might lose my job."

"Do what I say anyway, and I'll deal with that obstacle."

We don't have to remove the obstacles, that's God's responsibility. How He chooses to deal with the obstacles is also His responsibility. He may choose to do it in a way that makes us smile, or in a way that makes us sad, but our job is to go where He tells us. We are to put the right foot forward and obey His revealed will. As we take the next step, He promises to go before us to lead us into His will. Remember the goal, the destination? Colossians 1:9–10 reminds us that God wants us to be "filled with the knowledge of His will."

Which will? His revealed will or His concealed will? His will that He has already made known to us, or His "secret" will for our lives, containing all the future information we so cherish? Both, eventually! For one leads into the other. We find the concealed will on the road of His revealed will.

If we don't understand that, we can get a twisted view of God's nature. We picture Him saying to us at the end of our lives, "You should have known you were supposed to marry Susie, become an accountant at Parker Hannifin, have three children named Curly, Joe, and Moe, and retire to South Dakota; after all, I never told you."

As I sought to follow God's leading to go into ministry, I realized more and more that I needed to be serving others just as Jesus taught and modeled. At the same time I was wondering about God's wife for me. Attempting to be obedient to Him, I went to a little church where I was the only single for five years. I kept pointing out this obstacle to God, asking to know His secret will for my wife, I mean, life.

Several times I wanted to remove that obstacle myself and go to another church where there were more people my age. But I knew God had called me to serve, not to be served, so I stayed, trusting in His sovereignty. Then one day Annette walked into that tiny little church. (She was well worth the wait. If only she had married as well as I did.)

I found the concealed will of God for my life on the road of His revealed will. And you can't get there any other way. It takes only one wrong turn to make Colossians 1:9–10 read like this:

> We have not ceased to pray for you and to ask that you may be filled *a little* with the knowledge of His will, in *a little* spiritual wisdom and understanding, so that you may walk in a manner *somewhat worthy* of the Lord, to please Him in *a few respects*, bearing fruit in *isolated good works* and keeping *barely afloat* in the knowledge of God.

The fact is that we all make wrong turns, get off on the wrong foot, and then find ourselves hopelessly lost as it relates to God's will for our lives. The first step to take when that happens is to *read the directions again*. Then, admit you can't find the will of God from where you are. Something needs to change. So, retrace your steps, and let God deal with any obstacles that arise from your obedience. Admit that you can't get there from here. Are you tired of seeing rice fields in your spiritual life?

It's easy to get headed in the wrong direction in life, isn't it? And what can compound the issue is the many people we meet who are willing to give us directions. If we don't know what to do with our lives, they sure seem to. Some of them are reliable; many are not. Let's take a good look at this issue.

FOLLOW THROUGH

1. Is there any "secret, concealed" information that I've been expecting God to tell me? What is it?

2. A few of the areas where God has revealed His will to me already, but I haven't taken much action on are

   What might the possible implications of this situation be?

3. Sometimes my instincts and God's clear directions are at odds. What makes it so difficult to do what God has clearly told me to do?

4. If I'm to learn to trust my directions instead of my instincts, then I need to assess how well I know my directions. Psalm 37:31 says: "The law of his God is in his heart; his steps do not slip." What are the chances that the answer to some of my questions are already revealed in Scripture?

5. Can I think of a time in my life when I have taken a shortcut in life, feeling that this one little spiritual detour won't have much effect on the ultimate outcome of my life's direction? What effect did it have? Has its total effect had time enough to be felt?

6. What is an area in my life where I am currently on a detour, and need to retrace my steps to return to the road of obedience? Am I willing to go back and "retrace my steps" if I have taken a wrong turn in life?

7. What is the greatest obstacle in attempting to "retrace my steps"? Do I feel I can let God deal with that obstacle?

8. "I found the concealed will of God for my life on the road of His revealed will. And you can't get there any other way." I agree (or disagree) with this statement because

9. An "altered" version of Colossians 1:9–10 appears on page 63. Read it again and ask how much my life mirrors this altered version.

Making Contact

If you are involved in a detour from the revealed will of God, take this time alone with the Father to confess it to Him. Don't use flowery words, be brutally honest. If you are committed to retracing your steps, ask Him to strengthen you in your resolve. If you are wavering, wanting to retrace your steps, but afraid you don't have the strength, tell Him this too.

If there is no detour you are aware of in your life, ask God to make you aware of any that might be hidden from your understanding. Ask the Father to "[fill you] with the knowledge of His will in spiritual wisdom and understanding, so that you will walk in a manner worthy of the Lord."

CHAPTER FIVE

Can Thelma Tell Me God's Will?
Advice, Opinions, and the Will of God

At an NCAA cross-country championship held several years ago, the athletes were running along the prescribed route when they stumbled upon a perplexing choice. There were apparently two directions that looked reasonable. Unsure of which way to go, the crowded pack began to follow the front runners, who had made their choice. All, that is, except Mike Delcavo. He knew they were going the wrong way, and he tried to convince them of it.

As he started running in the opposite direction, and urging the rest to follow him, the majority of the runners ignored him, while others laughed at him. Only four other runners followed Delcavo, while the other 123 runners ran the other way. Of 128 runners, only Mike and four other runners chose the right direction.

Can you just picture those misguided runners, jockeying for position, drafting each other, sprinting at times, making all the right racing moves, yet the whole time they are headed in the wrong direction, moving further and further away from the finish line? Exhausted and spent, they ended the day realizing they had wasted their energy. All because the person they were trusting in to show them the right way failed them.

The front runners may have seemed more confident or self-assured, or sounded more authoritative when they told the other runners to follow them.

In the race of life, direction is everything. The people we listen to, and follow, will have a great impact on where we end up. The unfortunate situation is that there is no shortage of people who either knowingly or unknowingly will point us in the wrong direction, and then spur us on to run faster.

Finding the will of God is usually a multifaceted affair—that is, we discover the will of God not through one great experience, or one big road sign, but through a number of different means, all coming together to point in a specific direction. Each experience provides signs pointing in the right direction, but not necessarily to the final destination.

Part of our direction comes from the Bible. Where the Bible is silent about our need for direction, we get part of that direction through prayer, reflection, understanding our God-given design, and any number of other ways. But a pivotal way that must not be overlooked is through people, who for one reason or another we have come to trust or have sought out for advice.

In fact, a great deal of our direction in life is given through other people, therefore, it is one way in which God leads. The Bible tells us that "in abundance of counselors there is victory" (Proverbs 11:14; 15:22; 24:6). God encourages us to use this commonsense approach to gain the fullness of the knowledge of His will. "I don't doubt that the Holy Spirit guides your decisions from within when you make them with the intention of pleasing God," wrote C. S. Lewis. "The error would be to think that He speaks only within, whereas in reality He speaks also through Scripture, the Church, Christian friends, books, etc."[12] Yet, not all those we might seek out for advice are truly wise counselors. Which is why we must examine some of the pitfalls inherent in seeking the will of God through other people. Where we look, and to whom we look, for direction in life, are critical. Since our desire to know God's will for our life can at times be consuming, we are sometimes too eager to follow the direction of anyone who promises to give it. Thus, we need to consider some ideas that can help in this endeavor.

When Seeking God's Will with the Help of Others, Consider the Source

When I think of going to the wrong sources to find the will of God, King Saul comes to mind immediately. Saul was the very first king of Israel, handpicked by the people themselves. But his record was dismal. In fact, he had murdered priests, even the High Priest, and jealousy prompted him to make continual attempts on David's life.

Near the end of Saul's life the Philistines had gathered to make war on Israel, and when he saw their army, he was terrified. In his terror he turned to God. However, in keeping with his lifelong habit, he didn't turn to God in repentance and obedience, but only for desired information.

He had a question, a burning one. What would happen? How would it all turn out? In the past, at various times and in various situations, God had mercifully gone before him and enabled him to defeat his enemies for the sake of His people Israel. Now Saul wanted assurance, a guarantee, something he could pin his hopes on. But this time he had no such assurance.

We pick up the story in 1 Samuel 28:5–19:

> When Saul saw the camp of the Philistines, he was afraid and his heart trembled greatly. When Saul inquired of the LORD, the LORD did not answer him, either by dreams or by Urim or by prophets. Then Saul said to his servants, "Seek for me a woman who is a medium, that I may go to her and inquire of her." And his servants said to him, "Behold, there is a woman who is a medium at Endor."
>
> Then Saul disguised himself by putting on other clothes, and went, he and two men with him, and they came to the woman by night; and he said, "Conjure up for me, please, and bring up for

me whom I shall name to you." But the woman said to him, "Behold, you know what Saul has done, how he has cut off those who are mediums and spiritists from the land. Why are you then laying a snare for my life to bring about my death?" Saul vowed to her by the Lord, saying, "As the LORD lives, no punishment shall come upon you for this thing." Then the woman said, "Whom shall I bring up for you?" And he said, "Bring up Samuel for me." When the woman saw Samuel, she cried out with a loud voice; and the woman spoke to Saul, saying, "Why have you deceived me? For you are Saul." The king said to her, "Do not be afraid; but what do you see?" And the woman said to Saul, "I see a divine being coming up out of the earth." And he said to her, "What is his form?" And she said, "An old man is coming up, and he is wrapped with a robe." And Saul knew that it was Samuel, and he bowed with his face to the ground and did homage.

Then Samuel said to Saul, "Why have you disturbed me by bringing me up?" And Saul answered, "I am greatly distressed; for the Philistines are waging war against me, and God has departed from me and no longer answers me, either through prophets or by dreams; therefore I have called you, that you may make known to me what I should do." Samuel said, "Why then do you ask me, since the LORD has departed from you and has become your adversary? And the LORD has done accordingly as He spoke through me; for the LORD has torn the kingdom out of your hand and given it to your neighbor, to David. As you did not obey the LORD and did not execute His fierce wrath on Amalek, so the LORD has done this thing to you this day. Moreover the LORD will also give over Israel along with you into the hands of the Philistines, therefore tomorrow you and your sons will be with me. Indeed the LORD will give over the army of Israel into the hands of the Philistines!"

Saul, like so many others, set out to seek the will of God from people, but because of his lack of spiritual sensitivity to God, he hadn't felt the need to cultivate relationships with reliable and godly men who could assist him.

In times past, prophets, like Samuel, could tell him the will of God. But Samuel had died, and Saul's spiritual crutch had been removed. At other times, dreams were vehicles through which God would communicate His divine will, but Saul had no dreams. And then there was the third option, the Urim and Thummim.

The Urim and the Thummim were precious stones that were part of the ephod, the robe worn by the High Priest, which signified God's presence. No one knows exactly how they worked, whether the stones were cast like dice to determine God's will or whether God would simply speak through the High Priest while he wore them. In any case, all the normal ways to discover God's will on a matter were closed to Saul. Everything was quiet. He didn't know the will of God, and he didn't know anyone who could tell him.

Don't miss this situation. Saul had no great interest in obeying God, but he had an overwhelming fascination with discovering the will of God as it related to his future. So we read that Saul visited a medium, someone who was thought to be able to communicate with the dead.

Mediums were the equivalent of our modern-day palm or tarot readers and just as unreliable. However, God sovereignly intervened and allowed Samuel to return and speak with Saul, a miracle that surprised the medium herself.

Why did Saul go to a medium? What drove Saul to do what he had never done before, to a practice he had so opposed that he had outlawed it? Saul, so eager to ascertain the will or plan of God for his life, received what he desired. It just wasn't the plan he was hoping for. Perhaps there is a lesson to us about wanting to know too much.

DESPERATE AND AFRAID

When we are desperate and afraid we are far more vulnerable to advice we might otherwise ignore. It is in the future that our greatest fears live. For it is there that success or failure, marriage or divorce, health or death, happiness or calamity, fulfillment or discouragement, and myriads of other undetermined ends dwell.

We might casually glance at our horoscope. We start reading and depending upon that which we ordinarily would never consider. We start listening to people we have never consulted; people who don't share our biblical values or beliefs, but who seem confident and composed—everything that we, at the moment, are not.

I remember once visiting our county fair, and discovering nestled among the hundreds of booths one comfortably decorated like a living room with couches and easy chairs, and a sign over it that indicated that here you could get your palm read, and future told. My heart ached for the several individuals who were sitting and listening so very attentively to the "expert" dispense the future to them. The palm readers looked so friendly and poised, like psychologists talking to their patients.

What were the issues pressing on the hearts of those who stopped? What was so urgent that they would approach total strangers with their greatest fears and unanswerable questions, hoping that these people could give them the answers they couldn't find anywhere else? On a day when they had come just to unwind, have fun, and relax, their fears would not let them rest. Perhaps here they could get the direction and answers they sought, a small measure of peace. And what did they hear? What lies were they fed? What they were doing was going to cost them far more than the money they paid for this service.

They were being misled, lied to, and prompted to make significant decisions that could have resounding effects on their life. Was life so completely confusing to them that they would be reduced to this? But then, wasn't Saul at that point too?

Those giving advice will not be monsters with horns, spouting fire, but average, even pleasant, people telling you how easy it would be to "solve" your problem. They'll look and sound so confident about the direction you should go and the action you should take. And that's what you want, someone to give you some concrete guidance.

Who or what is the greatest source of authority in your life? Whose opinion weighs most heavily in your decisions? The answer might surprise you. Interestingly, God spoke to Saul, and He gave him the information he had been seeking, but it wasn't what he wanted to hear. This leads to the next principle for finding God's will.

Avoid Listening Only for What You Want to Hear

While on the one hand we face the danger of going to the wrong sources to find the will of God, an equally serious danger is ignoring the right voices because we can't accept the painful truth.

Can we seriously hope to ascertain the will of God for our lives by silencing those whom God might use to bring us His direction? Rehoboam, son and heir-apparent to Solomon, illustrates the consequences of turning a deaf ear to godly direction.

When Solomon, the great and wise king of Israel, died, he left a tremendous leadership vacuum. But his son Rehoboam tried to fill this vacuum. It was a daunting challenge, and many weren't sure he was up to it.

We can read about it in 1 Kings 12:1–11.

> Rehoboam went to Shechem, for all Israel had come to Shechem to make him king. Now when Jeroboam the son of Nebat heard of it, he was living in Egypt (for he was yet in Egypt, where he had fled from the presence of King Solomon). Then they sent and called him, and Jeroboam and all the assembly of Israel came and spoke to Rehoboam, saying, "Your father made our yoke hard; now therefore lighten the hard service of your father and his heavy yoke which he put on us, and we will serve you." Then he said to them, "Depart for three days, then return to me." So the people departed.

King Rehoboam consulted with the elders who had served his father Solomon while he was still alive, saying, "How do you counsel me to answer this people?" Then they spoke to him, saying, "If you will be a servant to this people today, and will serve them and grant them their petition, and speak good words to them, then they will be your servants forever." But he forsook the counsel of the elders which they had given him, and consulted with the young men who grew up with him and served him. So he said to them, "What counsel do you give that we may answer this people who have spoken to me, saying, 'Lighten the yoke which your father put on us'?" The young men who grew up with him spoke to him, saying, "Thus you shall say to this people who spoke to you, saying, 'Your father made our yoke heavy, now you make it lighter for us!' But you shall speak to them, 'My little finger is thicker than my father's loins! Whereas my father loaded you with a heavy yoke, I will add to your yoke; my father disciplined you with whips, but I will discipline you with scorpions.'"

At times we are more open to false input that flatters us than true information that may be uncomfortable or even painful. As a result we can give greater weight to anyone who will tell us what we want to hear, even if it isn't the truth. But by doing so we can silence the voices of those whom God would use to give us much-needed direction.

Rehoboam was such a case. What his young friends told him stroked his ego. He was a better man and a stronger man than his father, Solomon, they said. He needed to go out and show them what he was made of. That stroked Rehoboam's ego, and that was important to Rehoboam. It was what he wanted to hear.

Solomon's elders, on the other hand, were the men who had seen Rehoboam grow up, and they may have had a perspective about him that could have made Rehoboam feel uncomfortable.

Whenever I go back to my boyhood neighborhood I wince when I hear someone call me "little Danny Schaeffer." My old neighbors seldom resist the urge to tell an embarrassing story that strips me of my present accomplishments and titles. Any attempt at professional pretense is a wash. To them I will forever be "little Danny Schaeffer." And I never begrudge them that pleasure, because I know they love me and want only the best for my life.

Solomon's elders were only trying to give Rehoboam some advice that would have endeared him to the whole country. It seems apparent that the direction they gave Rehoboam would have made him a very effective leader, and that it was given to help him, not hurt him. In fact, they were pointing out a weakness in his father's approach, which if he seized it, would make him a more respected king. For, although Solomon was a wise and prosperous king, he wasn't perfect. His excesses, lavish and ostentatious, came primarily through taxation and forced labor.

Did they see in Rehoboam something of Solomon's penchant for using others to further his own ends? Did they recognize that while Rehoboam was probably a very capable man in his own right, he could never equal his father's accomplishments? Perhaps their advice was designed to quickly and effectively endear him to the people of Israel by portraying him as more sensitive to his people's burdens than his father had been.

God puts into our lives people who will speak truth to us: people who have perspective on our circumstances, and know us well enough to tell us the truth. Husbands, wives, parents, children, teachers, or mentors can reveal the truth about both us and our situations. Knowing the truth would launch us with great force into the direction God wants for our lives, according to His design.

Sometimes those people know us well enough to share ego-bruising information with us, and sometimes they won't be gentle about it. As a result, we may seek to avoid these people and their estimation of us. Rehoboam obviously had little regard for the elders' opinions. And when people like them tell us what we don't want to hear, listening can be painful. One can easily find reasons to discount their counsel.

On the other hand we may associate with people who think the way we do about things and share our same weaknesses. What they say makes us feel good; while it contradicts the advice of others whose truth is painful, it pumps us up. Rehoboam wasn't the last person to reject honest, wise counsel that could reveal to him the will of God because it came from unflattering lips. Today, helpful, healing, and divine messages designed to grow us up spiritually often come from the most unappealing of sources.

When truth comes in an unattractive package, and lies come beautifully wrapped, the choice is tough. And yet the decisions we make about who we listen to can be the most important choices we ever make. That's why when the only information we consider is positive information about ourselves, we are going to be blinded to God's will in certain areas.

Poor Rehoboam let an ego need drive his most important decision, and it made him deaf to the wise counsel that could have resulted in his becoming a wise and beloved leader.

HE CHOSE POORLY

One of the most critical choices we have to face in life is who we are going to listen to. That one decision will determine so much of our future. If we truly seek the will of God for our lives, we must accept the fact that it may at times lead to loneliness and separation from all that is comfortable. Our choice may lead to disturbing information about ourselves we wish we had never heard. And yet, the comfortable will sometimes lead us away from God's will, and the painful toward it. Rehoboam stood on the edge of greatness, but he chose to heed the wrong advice. It cost him ten of the twelve tribes of Israel.

> When all Israel saw that the king did not listen to them, the people answered the king, saying, "What portion do we have in David? We have no inheritance in the son of Jesse; to your tents, O Israel! Now look after your own house, David!" So Israel departed to their tents (1 Kings 12:16).

Only two tribes would follow Rehoboam all his days, the others followed someone else. He had made pivotal decisions based on the information that most appealed to him, not what was true.

His method of decision-making reminds me of that scene near the end of the movie *Indiana Jones and the Last Crusade* where both Indiana Jones and the villains have discovered the hiding place of the mythical Holy Grail, the vessel that supposedly gave one eternal life if one drank from it.

Within the secret room there are many different goblets—beautiful, ornate cups. The sentinel standing guard over the many drinking vessels asks the villain to choose first. After examining all the cups, he chooses the most beautiful vessel, the one most appealing to his vanity. Drinking from it, he begins aging hideously and turns to dust before our eyes. "He chose poorly," utters the sentinel sagely.

"He chose poorly"—that was Rehoboam's epitaph. The attractive and most alluring choice isn't always the best. Often it is the plainer and more difficult choice that leads to God's will.

Have we ever really addressed the importance of honesty before God and ourselves as we seek the will of God? Honesty about ourselves requires vulnerability to painful truth. But the truth is freeing, and can enable us for the first time to begin considering and dealing with reality—reality about who we are, what we are, and what God has designed us for. How can we expect God to lead us unless we are willing to accept the truth? Often the greatest obstacle to change in the lives of people is their inability to look at themselves honestly.

POWERING UP FOR A LETDOWN

When I was in seminary preparing for the pastorate, all the "successful" pastors of the day had charismatic personalities, dynamic presentation styles, and often, by their own admission, "driven personalities." These megapreachers had large congregations, tape ministries, and speaking engagements into the next millennium. Of course, I wasn't about to be outdone, so I made their achievements my goal and I went for it.

Upon graduation I started a church—primarily because no other church showed any interest in me. There I began to formulate visions of how things would turn out for me. I threw myself into my work and my goal of becoming a charismatic, dynamic pastor of a large congregation. Three years later my work threw me back up on the shores of reality. A real Jonah experience.

I had to face some painful truths about myself during that period, truths that would significantly impact my unstated but very real goals. First of all, I am not a charismatic personality. Truthfully, I'm quite a private person in a very public profession. I used a great deal of energy pretending to be charismatic when I wasn't. Imagine giving a skateboard a Corvette engine, and you get the picture. This was a painful reality for me to face, but a necessary one.

Second, I was not a "dynamic" speaker. Now I have never been accused of being boring, but the word *dynamic* doesn't fit me. My personality is more reflective in nature. If I am anything as a speaker, it is passionate. I believe in and care very deeply about the Scriptures I am preaching.

Finally, I was driven. I was driven to succeed, and motivated by a fear of failure. I put in eighty-hour weeks trying to create that unachievable reality I so desperately thought I needed. Unfortunately, as I learned, being driven isn't really a personality trait, it is the sin of ambition and selfishness run amuck.

Fortunately, reflective people can't be driven too long—they become intensely unhappy. I finally got tired of working and doing and keeping myself perpetually busy. I finally learned that I didn't need to do everything at church, and I didn't need to be the next megachurch pastor to be happy and fulfilled. I therefore didn't need to go to every meeting, and I even learned that others were far more gifted than I in many areas of church ministry. I just needed to stop obstructing some very gifted people and let them minister.

At the point I realized that, I began to smell the roses, spend more time with my wife and family, and enjoy life thoroughly. Ironically, I was also able to enjoy the ministry, which had become a grind.

Can you see how I was powering up for a mighty letdown? In my mind the will of God was connected to a dishonest self-appraisal. I could allow myself to be happy only if I achieved the things that I visualized, therefore those things I visualized had to be God's will; they just had to be! It never occurred to me that I might not have been designed for such a purpose.

Mercifully, some faithful Christians, many of them in my own church, came to my rescue. I remember one late-night discussion during some tumultuous times in the church when I was informed that a few people in our church accused me of being aloof. Completely unable to accept that assessment I shot back to the person who told me that, someone I greatly admired and trusted, "Well, do *you* think I'm aloof?"

The answer I was expecting was, "Of course not, Dan," and then I could dismiss the issue and get on with other things. But this person was strangely silent for a moment, and then said quietly and reluctantly, "Yeah, sometimes I think you are." I was stunned. I could tell it had been very difficult for this person to be so bluntly truthful. I think it hurt him as much to tell me, as it did for me to hear it. I tried to deny it inside, but over time I saw it was becoming true. Driven people tend to be aloof, because relationships impede speed, and speed is everything if you're driven. Life is a race, and relational pit stops consume too much time!

My friend was right (faithful are the wounds of a friend), but fortunately it wasn't a terminal condition. After it became clear to me that I wasn't charismatic, wasn't a dynamic speaker, and shouldn't even want to be driven, the will of God for me came into much clearer focus. I began to enjoy being me, and not trying to be like Chuck Swindoll, Stuart Briscoe, or Billy Graham. Furthermore, my congregation likes me just the way I am, and responds very graciously to my leading and teaching.

When I relaxed, and stopped holding churches captive to my private goals, we started to really have some fun. Parishioners became friends, and ministry stopped being mechanical, and started being more relational. I grew to love the people I once only led, and became a very fulfilled pastor. The only thing that changed was me.

I really believe that all anyone really wants out of life is to be happy and fulfilled. And since we're not sure how to get there we try all kinds of methods. We set these up as our goals and don't let anyone or anything get in our way of achieving them.

As a result we look for and listen to those folks who will tell us what we really want to hear—that everything we are chasing is worthwhile, and everything we are becoming is justified. We can't hear anything else because we're not listening for it. The truth for us is what we want to hear about ourselves, nothing else.

Yet in moments like this we can numbly parrot the prayers, "Lord, lead me into your will for my life." Sometimes God's will for our lives is delivered by folks without degrees in theology, with a fair share of weaknesses themselves, and in ways that make us feel uncomfortable.

Let's consider our own lives for a moment and ask some questions about those we listen to and lean on for advice. Maybe, if we ask these questions honestly, we can avoid choosing poorly.

ARE THOSE WHO HAVE YOUR EAR . . .

Spiritually Mature Believers?

The best way to get someplace is to ask someone who has been there and knows the way. Are we asking people to help us get somewhere they themselves have never been?

Please note that there is a distinct difference between "successful" and spiritually mature. One usually deals with giftedness, while the other always deals with proven character.

Successful people may often measure themselves by the yardstick of accomplishment, while spiritually mature people measure themselves by the yardstick of Christlikeness. Is the person who has your ear trying to make you successful—to measure you strictly by your accomplishments—or spiritually mature?

Honest about Themselves?

People who are not honest about themselves will not be honest with you or about you. Is the person you are listening to for advice and counsel practicing self-examination, or avoiding it? Cliques are often formed of people who behave similarly. Those who are not honest with themselves tend to congregate. It becomes a case of the blind leading the blind.

Are they free to speak of their failures and shortcomings? Are they personally open to painful truth, or are they "fountains of truth," dispensing their opinions to all who will listen?

Ego-Driven?

The greater one's ego, the less information one is able to accept about oneself. This person can only show us how he responded, not how we ought to choose. We can be asking direction of an ego-driven individual who simply has nothing to offer.

People who are driven by their egos constantly rehearse and rehash their strengths and victories, maybe even embellish them. If their trophies and awards and honors are continually on the tip of their tongue, they are demonstrating a strong need to have their own egos stroked. These folks may be wonderful people in many other ways, but they are unreliable navigators. Their compass is pointed continually in the wrong direction, so even with the best of intentions they can be dangerous to rely on for safe and honest direction.

Appealing to Your Sinful Nature?

Rehoboam's associates appealed to his darker side, his need for power, importance, and authority. We need to ask ourselves whether the information we are receiving from those who have our ear is appealing to us because it strokes our sinful nature.

At times even apparently mature Christians will encourage us to directly disobey God's clear command. If it will save money, stress, face, time, or any other urgent commodity, we will be encouraged to cut spiritual corners by those who have already done so. There will usually be a short-term payoff for this action, as they will point out.

Whoever appeals to your sinful nature is in no position to guide you into the will of God. Beating a hasty retreat is the order of the day.

The Kind of People You'd Like to Become?

We tend to take on the characteristics of those with whom we spend time. This can affect our future in significant ways. Are the people we are giving our ear to the kind of people we hope one day to become: people of character, maturity, and godliness? Their advice nine times out of ten will make us become more like them, act more like them, respond more like them. Is this what we really want? Are we comfortable with the decisions they have made, the direction their life is heading?

An integral part of discovering God's will for our lives is being prepared to hear unattractive, even painful, truths about ourselves. Honesty about ourselves is one of the quests we must be willing to embark upon if we hope to discover the will of God.

So after all is said and done, we sometimes do listen to and rely upon others for directions. They will often be significant factors in helping us to discern God's will and leading in our lives.

This chapter was written not to discourage you from listening to people, or even relying upon their advice. Rather, I hope it will provide some safe parameters to help you consider the reliability of your sources, as well as some painful truth you may encounter along the way.

And speaking of painful truth, what happens when we discover the will of God for our lives and it turns out to be a whole lot different than anything we'd expected? It can be shocking! Let's take a look.

FOLLOW THROUGH

1. Can I recall a time in my life when I found myself going to the wrong sources to discover the will of God? What (or who) was the wrong source? How did I discover that the advice was wrong?

2. Who or what was the bad connection that I had the *hardest time* breaking off? Why?

3. Is there anyone or anything I am listening to today that I am beginning to believe might just be a "bad connection"? (Discuss as a group some possible bad connections to help us think beyond our own list.)

4. What made me susceptible to the bad connections in my life?

5. One of the reasons we go to the wrong sources is because we're desperate and afraid. Is this my experience? Explain.

6. Can I remember a time when fear and curiosity has prompted me to listen to people I would ordinarily have ignored? (Share an example.)

7. Sometimes I feel, like Saul, that all the usual channels of discovering the will of God are closed. Agree or disagree. Why?

8. The last time I found myself, like Saul, seeking direction instead of repentance, was when

9. Do I remember a time when an ego need in my life caused me to make a decision I later regretted?

10. Who were the people in my past whose advice I wish I had listened to? What did not listening to them cost me?

11. When truth comes in an unattractive, and sharp-edged package, and lies come beautifully wrapped and make us feel good all over, the choice is tough. Can I think of an experience in my life that confirms this statement?

12. What "painful truths" have I had to come to grips with in my own life?

13. Who are the people in my life who have my ear? Are they spiritually mature believers, honest about themselves, the kind of people I want to become like?

Making Contact

Has God been trying to tell you something through others? What truth about yourself do you keep hearing from other people, but resist?

Take a few quiet moments of reflection and ask God to help you be honest with yourself. Prepare yourself by asking Him for the courage to do this, as it can be a frightening prospect. Ask close friends, relatives, or members of the group to help you in this time of self-reflection.

Ask God to help you remember how hearing the truth about yourself in the past has helped you grow spiritually and emotionally. Focus on the growth and maturity this step could bring to your life. Where will you be in six months, a year, two years, if you take this courageous step?

CHAPTER SIX

Boy, Did I Get a Wrong Number! Dealing with the Unexpected and Unwelcome Will of God

Years ago, Goldie Hawn starred in a movie called *Private Benjamin.* The movie was about a woman who, to escape the pain in her life, joined the army. While she was being recruited she was shown pictures of Maui and other exotic destinations, places she was assured she would see and visit. The unscrupulous recruiter described beautiful condos she would live in, and before long she signed up.

My favorite scene in the movie comes when she has been introduced to the real army—boot camp. Miserable, she is marching around in a circle outside in the rain with other recruits, and saying to herself, "I want the *other* army: the condos and the beaches." It's hilarious because we all can identify with desperately wanting to get something, and then, after getting it, finding out it's not what it was cracked up to be. For Private Benjamin the real army was unwelcome and unexpected.

Sometimes the will of God can be like that. We were absolutely sure that if God would just reveal His will to us, we would be delighted to receive the news. But sometimes the will of God ends up being unexpected and unwelcome. Then we find ourselves saying, "I want the *other* will of God: the manna, and the miracles, and the smiting of the Philistines."

The Bible tells us that a fellow named Jonah had a very similar problem. Jonah, like Moses, received a clear, supernatural revelation of God's will for his life. "The word of the Lord," it says in chapter 1 verse 1, literally "came to Jonah." It doesn't say he was even looking for it.

Think about it: The bush was burning for Jonah, and he didn't have to use one match. The problem was that instead of removing his sandals and warming to the fire, Jonah got cold feet. Poor Jonah; he wanted to extinguish the burning bush, but he couldn't.

What happens when, instead of being in the dark about God's will, we are enlightened—but disappointed? In other words, the will of God has become clear to us, but we try to escape it.

Sometimes knowing the will of God can be a lot harder than not knowing it, because knowing the will of God can often be a two-edged sword. We don't always want to know all the will of God, do all the will of God, hear all the will of God, or even endure all the will of God.

Paul Tournier reminds us, "If we read the Old Testament Prophets we see that sometimes . . . the will of God is that everything should be destroyed, that the cup of sin be drained to the dregs, so as to make possible a resurrection. We find it hard to understand the detours along which God takes us, and it is often only afterwards that we see that we had to go that way."[13]

GOD'S WILL, JONAH'S WAY

The story of Jonah is a familiar one to many readers of the Bible. Jonah was a prophet of God who, upon discovering God's will for him was to go to Nineveh, promptly packed his bags for Tarshish.

There was a reason for this: Jews *hated* Ninevites.

Nineveh was a wicked city, and God wanted them to know of His displeasure and judgment. In that day, only the great Babylon was a more powerful city than Nineveh. Furthermore, because of Israel's disobedience and unfaithfulness, God had sent prophets telling them that they would be judged, and the agent of that judgment would be the dreaded Assyrians. Assyria was a rising world power, destined to destroy Israel, and Nineveh was the capital of Assyria. Jonah understood all of this; thus we read:

> The word of the LORD came to Jonah the son of Amittai saying, "Arise, go to Nineveh the great city and cry against it, for their wickedness has come up before Me." But Jonah rose up to flee to Tarshish from the presence of the LORD. So he went down to Joppa, found a ship which was going to Tarshish, paid the fare and went down into it to go with them to Tarshish from the presence of the LORD (Jonah 1:1–3).

Jonah didn't want to go because he was secretly afraid that when he preached their need for repentance, they might actually repent; then God, because He was merciful, wouldn't judge them. Jonah *wanted* God to judge them, because if He did, they couldn't be used to judge Israel. But what Jonah didn't understand was that God had two reasons for sending him to Nineveh: one was for Nineveh, and the other was for Jonah himself.

The story is a familiar one: Jonah tries to run from God's will for him, and books passage on a boat headed in the opposite direction. A storm brews over the Mediterranean, and the crew, finally convinced the storm was due to the displeasure of Jonah's God, eventually agrees to throw him into the sea. He would have drowned in the roiling waves, but God saves him by sending a large fish to swallow him. He lives for three days in the belly of the fish.

In chapter 3 the disobedient prophet finally and reluctantly fulfills the will of God and preaches to Nineveh that God is going to destroy them in forty days because of their wickedness. And, you guessed it, they did the unthinkable. They repented. They humbled themselves before God, and God, seeing this act, did not destroy them, which was what Jonah had been preaching God was going to do. Chapter 4 verse 1 sums up Jonah's mood over this whole affair in a definite understatement:

> It greatly displeased Jonah, and he became angry.

This chapter in the book of Jonah can teach us a lot about the will of God, especially when we're faced with unexpected and unwelcome events in our lives. Jonah was fully prepared, and probably eager to preach destruction to Nineveh; that would have been easier. But in the back of Jonah's mind he had some reasons for not wanting to do the will of God. And these excuses for not obeying God's revealed will haven't changed much over the years; we still use them today. Let's take a look at several:

EXCUSE #1

God's Will Might Let Someone Else off the Hook

> He prayed to the LORD and said, "Please LORD, was not this what I said while I was still in my own country? Therefore, in order to forestall this . . ." (Jonah 4:2).

Forestall what? Forestall their judgment? No, forestall their *repentance*. Jonah didn't want to let them off the hook. He just had a sinking feeling they would repent and God would be merciful to them. At times we don't want to do God's will because God's will means forgiveness, reconciliation, patience, and love: the very things we are rebelling against at the moment. We think we'd be letting someone who doesn't deserve it off the hook.

One of my most tragic memories is that of a young man I met and befriended several years ago. He was in the military, and had a gut-wrenching story to tell, a story seemingly straight out of Hollywood.

He had a best friend, one he confided in, went everywhere with, spent all his time with, and trusted in implicitly. Then he fell in love with a girl and they got married. After a while they had a son. Life couldn't have been better for this young man; he had a best friend, a wife, and an adorable son. The best friend joined the family in everything, becoming a surrogate member of the family. But one day the husband came home to find his wife in bed with his best friend.

This began a nightmare in which his wife divorced him and married his best friend; both of his best friends and his son became alienated from him. As is so often the case, bitterness ruled both sides, but it was especially acute in this young man. I have never met a man so consumed with bitterness. Everything he did and said was related to his bitterness over this situation.

When I first met him he was bright, articulate, and polite. But as he told his story, he became bitter, ugly, and malicious. Hatred had eaten away at his life, leaving only a shell of a man. As we counseled I probed and discovered that his marriage had been troubled almost from the start, contrary to what he had made himself believe. Only one thing could salvage his life and relationship with his son: forgiveness.

This he wouldn't do. He adamantly refused every time. He was a staunch churchgoer and was willing to do anything else God might ask of him, but not this—not ever. For his own sake, for his future, I pleaded with him to let go of his bitterness. But he wouldn't, because he was afraid that by doing so he would be letting those who had hurt him so deeply "off the hook." I tried to convince him that he was the only one on the hook, and it was he who would be set free, but my counsel fell on deaf ears. He quit coming to church, and I can only hope he eventually found freedom through forgiveness.

God's will was crystal clear to Jonah; there was no room for doubt, but this was no small issue to Jonah. We were talking about forgiving *Ninevites*. Therefore, though the will of God could be shown to him clearly and unmistakably, it was nevertheless unwelcome, and never embraced.

Sometimes we resist doing something we know God wants us to do because we're afraid it would let someone off the hook. Is there a Ninevite in your life? Is there someone who has or is hurting you badly, and therefore you resist forgiving that person? Join the ranks! At some time in our lives, we all have a Ninevite on whom God wants us to have mercy! Could it be that this issue is the one God is most concerned about in your life? This step could open up the doors to many other things, but if we won't take it, it could close the doors to everything else while God presses the issue.

EXCUSE #2

Someone Will Get Something Good They Don't Deserve

Those Ninevites didn't deserve Jonah's grace—oh, excuse me—God's grace. Sometimes it's easy to confuse those two isn't it? Jonah wasn't afraid to deliver God's judgment, but he didn't want to have to be an instrument of His grace. Jonah didn't mind God's forgiving and delivering *him* from death, he just didn't want the Ninevites to get the same treatment.

In California (where I live), as in many places in America, the demographics of our society are changing almost daily. About fifty or more years ago a number of wonderful churches were founded in our area. They were strong, with wonderful ministries and out-reaches. Most of their members were white, middle-class people. But over time the areas surrounding these churches have changed. "White flight" has left many of these churches in changing ethnic neighborhoods. Once booming and thriving, these churches' mem-berships have dwindled. It is not uncommon to see thirty or forty elderly saints gathered in sanctuaries designed to hold five or six hundred.

But the area is now largely African-American or Hispanic or Asian, and the style and ministry of the established church do not appeal to them. By the sovereign will of God, thriving ministries are now popping up among these groups, but they sorely lack buildings. Unfortunately, with these new ethnic groups have come gangs and violence. While these elements are never the majority of the people of any race, they are often the most visible. So, many older congre-gations in decline face agonizing decisions. Do they open their doors to these new ministries, and take a back seat in the church they founded and built? What about the bad elements of that ethnic group? It is so much easier to love sinners who don't look and act like—well, sinners.

Do these groups deserve the beloved saints' building? Unquestionably the Great Commission reaches out to these new ethnic groups, but the emotions surrounding the issue are volatile at times. And today there is more than just "white flight," there is "black flight" and "brown flight"; increasingly there will be new groups fleeing areas and churches, while others follow them in.

Ninevites can come to us in all shapes and colors, can't they? When we look at others as a threat, it is difficult to extend the mercy of God to them. Interestingly, when we are afraid that doing God's will might let someone off the hook, we are showing that we resent God's mercy. When we are afraid that doing God's will might allow people to get something they don't deserve, we are showing we actually resent His grace.

EXCUSE #3

What About Our Reputation?

Jonah, I think, felt very embarrassed at God's actions. Here he had gone and threatened God's judgment, and it never came. Could Jonah have felt that he had a little egg on his face, and God had put it there? Jonah must have thought about how all this reflected on him.

Being humbled before someone is a terribly uncomfortable position to be in, especially if you don't have high regard for the person to begin with. It can be easy to ignore the clear will of God, and justify ourselves, if our reputation is on the line. When God's will is for us to smite the Philistines that is one thing, but when it is His will for us to help save the Ninevites, that is quite another.

When a woman is in a marriage and has lost all respect for her husband, the will of God for her to respect him is hard to fulfill. It is hard because he has become a Ninevite to her. To show respect to someone you feel respect for is quite an easy command to fulfill, but to show respect for a Ninevite is a tall order. But at times, that is the will of God. And at times it is unexpected and unwelcome. The command becomes something we want to avoid altogether. We are willing to address any other aspects of the will of God for us, but just not *this* one.

I have known many people who, because of pride, have not obeyed the clear leading of God to respect, or forgive, or be patient with, or honor, a Ninevite near them—including yours truly. They are all packed and ready to go to Tarshish and would do anything God wants them to do there, but just not in Nineveh. Why, they ask, would God want them to do such a thing? It doesn't make any sense, and they just know it won't work, or do any good. Why, why, why? This Ninevite could be your spouse, or a parent, or an employer, or have authority over you in some other way.

That question leads us into the two reasons why I believe God often wants us to do things that are unexpected and unwelcome in our lives.

REASON #1

God's Direction Is Our Prescription

Jonah's journey to Nineveh was not only God's clear direction, it was Jonah's clear prescription. Jonah thought his journey and commission to go to Nineveh was all for the benefit of the Ninevites whom he disliked, so he was understandably reluctant. After all, Jonah didn't need to repent; the Ninevites did. But he was wrong. God could have used anybody to go to Nineveh, but he chose Jonah, and for good reason. Jonah had an illness of the soul, a malady of the heart, and the prescription for it was Nineveh.

Nineveh was Jonah's medicine. A friend of mine once had to have a brain tumor removed. This is very delicate surgery, and this woman wanted the best medical experts and surgeons she could find. There was just such a group of doctors in Los Angeles, but she had to fight with her insurance company to get the chance to see them. This was the place she knew she could get her problem dealt with most effectively.

With all her heart she wanted to go there, and she asked us to intercede in prayer for her. When her prayer was answered, these experts proceeded to cut her head open with a sharp instrument and probe near her brain to remove a tumor the size of a baseball. Afterward there was pain from the surgery itself, discomfort from medication, and even scars. Yet, she gladly fought for this opportunity, because in the end it brought healing.

In the same way, Nineveh was the place of healing for Jonah. No other town was quite like Nineveh, not so brash, not so evil, not so sinful, not so sadistic in its treatment of its captives. Living in a border town, Jonah had undoubtedly heard firsthand of its evil and atrocious behavior. And yet, the cure for Jonah, and his character, would come only when he preached God's judgment and grace in the evil streets of that city. The whole idea was distasteful to Jonah, something he never would have volunteered for.

God had some lessons in store for Jonah in Nineveh that he never would have expected.

Have we considered how frequently God's direction for our lives, His clear will, is not only our direction, but also our prescription? The thing that we rebel most against doing is the thing we most need to do.

AN ANTIDOTE TO POISON

When God calls us to forgive the person we most want to punish, our directions are also our prescriptions. We're bitter, and we need healing. Something is eating away at us, and only in the difficult and unwelcome will of God can we find healing.

From the most poisonous plants in the world we often find the antidotes for some of our worst diseases and conditions. Taken in the right amounts these poisonous plants become our salvation. It is from the venom of the rattlesnake that a lifesaving antidote is created. The venom, mixed and balanced with other ingredients, is absolutely essential to counteracting the lethal effects of the snakebite. Through nature itself we learn the strange and paradoxical reality that we can find healing from the most unlikely of sources.

When God calls us to reach out to those we would most naturally ignore or even disdain, our directions also contain our prescriptions. When a heart is hard and stiff, it needs to be softened. We need to look at these people through the eyes of God, not through our own eyes.

I remember the wife of a pastor talking about a mission she was involved with in Washington, D.C. Their church tried to enlist volunteers to feed and care for the down-and-out. Some went and loved it, but she had a particularly good friend whom she had constantly tried to enlist. Time after time, the friend made excuses for not going. Finally, reluctantly, she agreed to go. That day she served dozens of homeless and forgotten people in a food line. When the day was done the pastor's wife, understandably curious, asked her friend how she felt about the experience. The woman bluntly said that she would never do it again. Surprised and saddened, the pastor's wife asked her why. Her reply was honest, but sad. "Because they don't appreciate what we're doing for them."

The pastor's wife then contrasted her friend's attitude with that of a woman who volunteered regularly. Every day this particular woman, before she went in to serve meals to these homeless people, would pray, "Lord, today You will pass before me in that line, help me to treat You with kindness and dignity." That volunteer found her prescription in her direction. This service, for her, was not about whether or not someone appreciated it; it was simply an act of love, born of the Lord who loved her. How someone might react to her act of love was not her concern. She was a Christian in the process of becoming daily more like Christ.

When God's will for us is to endure that which we would most naturally seek to escape, our directions are also our prescriptions. In these moments the will of God can often seem unexpected and unwelcome. We suddenly discover that we're not going to put our enemies to flight, we aren't going to cross the Red Sea on dry land, we are instead being called to a difficult task for which there may be no recognizable reward.

James describes this situation eloquently in James 1:2–4.

> Consider it all joy, my brethren, when you encounter various trials, knowing that the testing of your faith produces endurance. And let endurance have its perfect result, that you may be perfect and complete, lacking in nothing.

Don't miss the key—there is to all of these trials a desired perfect result. The result is the completion of that which was incomplete, "that you may be perfect and complete, lacking in nothing." When Jonah compared himself to the Ninevites, who were admittedly some of the most evil people ever to disgrace the pages of history, it would have been hard to convince him that they could play any part in shaping his character.

Corrie ten Boom, author of *The Hiding Place*, and a survivor of a concentration camp in Nazi Germany during World War II, knew well that God sometimes uses strange means to hone the character of His people. She had endured many "dark times" in her life. But she had also learned valuable lessons about her God. "When a train goes through a tunnel," she wrote, "you don't throw away your ticket and jump off. You sit still and trust the engineer."[14]

God saw that Jonah lacked something, and the antidote was Nineveh. The idea that from the poison of the Assyrians could come any improvement in his own condition was unthinkable.

We are often afflicted with this same idea. God could never use my husband, wife, parents, employer, children, teacher, neighborhood, _____ (you fill in the blank), to shape my character. The idea of using those who seem poisonous to us to help mold our character is unthinkable. Being saved from the deadly effects of venom by venom? Impossible! Developing a cure for my condition from the most poisonous person in my life? Never! Yet does not the Word of God tell us that God's wisdom and ways are unfathomable?

> Oh, the depth of the riches both of the wisdom and knowledge of God! How unsearchable are His judgments and unfathomable His ways! FOR WHO HAS KNOWN THE MIND OF THE LORD, OR WHO BECAME HIS COUNSELOR? (Romans 11:33–34).

When God gives us directions, when the word of the Lord is as clear to us as it was for Jonah, those directions are also our prescriptions. God sees a need in our lives that can be met only when we respond to His clear leading. He also knows that this will be met by our resistance, but as in the case of Jonah, He will not relent. Why? The answer is found in the second reason.

REASON #2

Resisting God's Direction Interrupts Our Spiritual Development; Yielding to His Will Leads Us to Spiritual Growth

Take another look at Jonah.

> It greatly displeased Jonah, and he became angry. He prayed to the LORD and said, "Please LORD, was not this what I said while I was still in my own country? Therefore in order to forestall this I fled to Tarshish, for I knew that You are a gracious and compassionate God, slow to anger and abundant in lovingkindness, and one who relents concerning calamity. Therefore now, O LORD, please take my life from me, for death is better to me than life." The LORD said, "Do you have good reason to be angry?" (Jonah 4:1–4).

Jonah became bitter, resentful, and eventually genuinely suicidal. Why? Because he had a cold, bitter, and ugly heart. As he toured that great city of Nineveh he saw people, thousands of them—lost, blind, and hopeless people—and all he wanted was to see them destroyed. He could see them only as enemies; prejudice blinded his eyes to seeing them any other way. From his perspective they were only nuisances who should be removed from his life. He was so spiritually sick that he didn't even want them to repent and turn to God. He wanted them dead.

Can you see what his resistance to God's unexpected and unwelcome will was doing to him? In verse 2 he claims to know God, "for I knew that You are a gracious and compassionate God," but did he really? Jonah's heart and God's heart simply weren't beating together. Jonah was love-impaired, compassion-challenged; God was "slow to anger and abundant in lovingkindness."

ENFORCING THE PRESCRIPTIONS

Jonah's spiritual development had stopped. God wanted to lead him to the cure for his spiritual apathy, and that meant Nineveh for Jonah. Jonah was like a dying patient whose doctor has the cure, but the patient refuses the cure, because he doesn't agree with the diagnosis that he is really dying. But our Great Physician will enforce His prescriptions. As He did with Jonah, God will make us take our medicine. We are His children, and He will not allow us to remain sickly.

Often, the medicine we most need is the aspect of God's will that we most strongly resist. God didn't want merely to heal the Ninevites' condition, He wanted to heal Jonah's. This wasn't simply a Ninevite issue anymore, it was a heart issue between God and Jonah. God's will wasn't simply that Jonah preach to the Ninevites, but that he sense their lostness and blindness, that he begin to care as deeply for them as God did.

Stubbornness over accepting the will of God can become a consuming and destroying passion. Sometimes it seems that, like Jonah, we'd rather go to our grave than give in. Jonah was so upset over what God had clearly called him to do that he allowed it to sap from him all the pleasure of living. He had so immersed himself in his anger over the outcome that he had squeezed all the joy out of life.

I know too many Christians who have allowed all the joy to be squeezed from life because of their bitterness over a difficult step God has clearly called them to take. They become Jonahs: sulking, stubborn, and resentful of God's unexpected and unwelcome will.

What He calls them to accept, they insist on rejecting.

When He calls them to understand, they insist on criticizing.

Where He calls them to see their own character flaws, they can only focus on others' weaknesses.

When we resist God's clear will, we stop our own spiritual development. This is why we can seem so mature and knowledgeable in certain areas of life, and yet such babies in others. Jonah had an immature heart, it wasn't fully developed, and the Ninevites were what he needed to get it growing again.

Yet, he was a prophet of God, knew a lot of theological information about God, and could articulate it clearly enough to affect an entire city for God. In his knowledge he was mature; in his application of that knowledge he was an infant. He didn't mind God being gracious and compassionate, slow to anger, abundant in lovingkindness, and relenting concerning calamity, *as long as it wasn't toward the Ninevites.*

CURES SOMETIMES HURT

In chapter 4 of Jonah, the prophet is sitting on a hill overlooking Nineveh. As the heat of the day increased God raised up a plant to be shade for him. This tickled Jonah's fancy, and he was very happy about it. But then God sent a worm to destroy the plant, and it withered. Jonah was mad again. How dare God destroy that plant that he loved so much! God must be cruel and uncaring. Ironically, this was precisely what God had been trying to show Jonah about his own ailment. Jonah cared about the plant, but he didn't care about Ninevites. And he couldn't understand why God did.

Many of our responses to God are based not on what He reveals of Himself, but our latest experience with Him. Our attitudes toward God resemble a child's attitude toward going to the doctor. Recently we were caring for a couple's children and took them out to dinner at a well-known fast-food establishment. While there, playing on the playground, their little daughter cut her foot rather badly. She was in great pain, and we could tell something was lodged in her foot, so we whisked her off to the doctor's office.

The doctor knew immediately there was a piece of glass in her foot that had to be removed, or it would ultimately lead to serious problems. The cure was simple: remove the glass.

Yet, removing the glass hurt, because she had to have a shot to anesthetize the area, and that was painful. All Tiffany knew was that her foot hurt, and that the cure hurt too.

We sometimes wonder why our cures have to hurt so much, and the reason is often that our condition was far worse than we imagined. Something was in us that needed to be removed, and the removal involves pain. It could be an idea, a false trust, a misplaced hope, or a myriad of other things.

Our perception of God is often directly traceable to our latest encounter with the Great Physician. Sometimes we just need some good advice: lose weight, exercise, eat sensibly. When such advice comes, we perceive God to be a kindly physician whom we trust and love implicitly. But when our condition is more serious, and we need a more painful or radical treatment, our perception of God changes dramatically.

Jonah wasn't well; his heart was diseased. But God loved him too much to leave him that way. And God loves us too. We are all Jonahs in at least one area of our lives, but, like Jonah, we can be ignorant of it. Who are our Ninevites? What is our Nineveh? Where is our Nineveh?

What handicap might we be seeking to ignore? What area of our spiritual development might be stopped? If we are serious about discovering the will of God, we must be ready to accept its unexpected and unwelcome aspects. As strange as it may seem at the moment, even when it hurts God is trying to squeeze joy into our lives, through an antidote to a character deficiency, which is slowly siphoning it away.

Yet, many of us have the same attitude toward God as we do toward our family doctor: we trust His intentions, but fear His methods. God's methods may seem strange, but it's only because we cannot see the whole picture as He sees it. Let Him cure you of Ninevitis!

FOLLOW THROUGH

1. Here is a list of people, places, and circumstances I've come to realize are definitely the will of God for my life, but they are (or were) unexpected and unwelcome.

2. "Sometimes knowing the will of God can be a lot harder than not knowing it." Agree or disagree. Why?

3. What are some areas where I'm not sure I *want* to know the will of God (because it might not be what I want to hear)?

4. Have I ever been afraid that doing God's will might let someone off the hook? Explain.

5. Sometimes I don't want to do the will of God because I'm afraid someone will get something they don't deserve (forgiveness, acceptance, love). Can I think of any examples from my own life?

6. Has doing the will of God ever threatened my reputation? What was my reaction? What was the result?

7. The last time God's clear direction was also my prescription for life was the time when . . . . (Explain how the direction brought healing.)

8. "Stubbornness over accepting the will of God can become a consuming and destroying passion." Do I really believe this is true? Why or why not?

9. Name some people in your life who may seem "poisonous" to you now, but may be used of God to bring healing to your life.

Making Contact

Earlier in this chapter I wrote, "Many of us have the same attitude toward God that we do toward our family doctor: we trust His intentions, but fear His methods." If there is any truth to this in your own life, you need to do some business with God. If you indeed fear God's methods, you need to speak with Him about it. The honesty can't hurt, in fact it can only help your relationship. Meditate on Jeremiah 29:11–13: "'For I know the plans that I have for you,' declares the LORD, 'plans for welfare and not for calamity to give you a future and a hope. Then you will call upon Me and come and pray to Me, and I will listen to you. You will seek Me and find Me when you search for Me with all your heart.'" Our God does not change, and His plans are the same for you today as they have always been. Be sure you embrace this truth before you explore God's will any further.

CHAPTER SEVEN

If It Feels Right, Do It—
And Other Christian Fables

Obedience is the key to all doors: feelings come (or don't come) and go as God pleases. We can't produce them at will, and musn't try.

—C. S. LEWIS[15]

One year I was leading a men's discipleship group that was discussing a section in a book about God's will. The author gave some helpful hints on this difficult subject of trying to find the will of God, but at the end he recognized that there is often an intangible factor involved in the process; namely, our feelings.

So, attempting to explain this intangible, and give practical advice on the subject, he wrote, "Anytime your 'gut' leaves you feeling unsettled you can be 100 percent certain it is not of God. The Holy Spirit is not the author of confusion. Satan, however, is." The publishers placed this quote in bold letters on the page, so it could not be missed.

Everyone who read this statement reigned up at this notion. We all recognized the danger of allowing our feelings to determine what is of God and what is not. We recognized that the source of our "gut" feeling is often difficult to decipher. While the Holy Spirit is not the author of confusion, and Satan is, can we always tell who (or what) authored our current feelings? I know I can't!

Now I want to be quick to say that the author of the book we were considering is a godly man, and the rest of what he had to say was very helpful. But I think his statement highlights our struggle to determine what part our feelings play in understanding God's will for our lives.

Pastor and author Erwin Lutzer has correctly discovered that "a Christian life based on feeling is headed for a gigantic collapse." I invite you to think along with me as we examine some principles in Scripture that can create some varying and even contradictory feelings, with the hope that we may avoid a "gigantic collapse."

Let's look first at Proverbs 3:5–6 where, if we look carefully, we will discover:

Sometimes the Will of God Feels Confusing

What does it mean to "trust in the Lord with all your heart, and do not lean on your own understanding"? It means just what it says. Some aspects of the will of God produce the feeling of confusion in us. When Jesus got on His knees before His disciples and washed their feet, they were confused. Peter, in fact, was terribly confused. A master washing the feet of His disciples? Unheard of, illogical. And then Jesus said, "I want you to do this for each other, because the greatest among you shall become the servant of all. Just trust me on this, Peter, you won't understand it all now, but you will later."

We know that truth didn't originally register with them, in fact, it felt confusing to them. It was a countercultural command with no precedent. Yet, it was clearly the will of God. Sometimes the will of God will create in us feelings of confusion. Our "gut" feeling will not be understanding, but a great big question mark.

Sometimes the Will of God Feels Terrifying

Daniel in the lions' den, Shadrach, Meshach, and Abed-nego in the fiery furnace, the early church under persecution for sharing the gospel, Stephen being stoned for his faith—all were doing the will of God, yet each one must have felt fear, a very powerful emotion. Jesus, as He faced the prospect of the cross in Gethsemane, felt agony as He contemplated the fate that awaited Him, yet He was perfectly within the will of God.

Years ago, while I was still in college, I was asked to give my testimony on a public stage, on the campus of Saddleback Junior College. We were preparing to start an outreach there, and a concert, with our testimonies, was part of our advertisement for the outreach. These testimonies would be given while the students were between classes, and at a place where many would be gathered.

I was picked.

I was surprised.

I was *scared*!

Why? Because I was going to be attending this school the next semester, and I knew I would be pigeonholed as the school's religious fanatic before I even arrived. I didn't mind giving my testimony, I just didn't want to do it in front of anyone!

Several days before I was going to share my testimony I was frequently stricken with bouts of overwhelming fear. On the morning I was to share my testimony I couldn't eat. Ten minutes before I was going to share I was praying for the rapture, an earthquake, a short in the sound system, anything. Then the time came. I was introduced and stepped up onto the platform like a man approaches the hangman's noose.

I remember only a little of what I said, because I was mostly numb during this time. When I got done and turned to walk away, you could have heard a pin drop. I figured this was what it must feel like to die. Then, suddenly, the place erupted in applause and I looked back to see smiling faces, contemplative faces, and faces that said simply, "That took courage." When I hit the bottom of the stage, exhilaration overwhelmed me.

I knew God had called me to share my testimony, and yet, if I had gone by my "gut feeling" I would have bowed out. Because, if the truth be known, sometimes the will of God feels *terrifying*.

Sometimes the Will of God Feels Great

As recorded in Luke 10, Jesus appointed seventy disciples, in addition to the Twelve, and sent them out with instructions to preach the kingdom of God to the people of Israel, and He gave them power to heal and cast out demons. In verse 17 we read, "The seventy returned with joy, saying, 'Lord, even the demons are subject to us in Your name.'"

Wow! Can you imagine being given that kind of power and seeing it used through your life? Those disciples were pumped! There are moments like that in our lives when we say what we feel God wants us to, and the person listens and changes. We share our faith, and someone believes, we take a stand for Jesus, and get affirmed.

I remember the first time I ever led someone to faith in Christ. I was in high school and our church high school youth sponsor had challenged us to tell our friends that we were Christians. This was hard for me, because I honestly enjoyed the secret of having a relationship with Christ. It was like a precious secret between me and God.

But in obedience I shared with a good friend why I went to church, and what it did for me. I didn't share a gospel outline, because I didn't know that such a thing existed. I left out important information, and said things that weren't necessary at all. I muffed the whole process—and led my friend to Christ all the same. I was blissfully ignorant. I simply did what God asked me to do, and people became Christians—what a concept! Sometimes it just feels great to do the will of God. If it felt this good all the time, life would be much easier, but alas, that's not always the case.

Sometimes the Will of God Feels Like Deprivation

Paul reminds us in 1 Thessalonians that "this is the will of God, your sanctification; that is, that you abstain from sexual immorality"

(1 Thessalonians 4:3). Sometimes the will of God means denying yourself some sensual pleasure, and at that time the will of God feels like deprivation. God seems like a cosmic killjoy. There are books you can't read, movies you shouldn't see, words you shouldn't use, and places you shouldn't go!

When our son Andrew was about seven years old, a movie was shown on a Friday afternoon for his class; it was a reward for good school work. But a teacher had unwittingly allowed the showing of a movie that was inappropriate, and Andrew knew he wasn't allowed to watch. It had swearing, sexual innuendo, occultic themes, and was just plain scary for a seven-year-old. Andrew knew he wasn't supposed to watch the movie, so as it began, he went to the teacher and said quietly, "I'm not allowed to watch this movie."

Andrew was sent to study hall for the remainder of the time. His father's will was very clear, but in doing my will he had to stick out, and miss out. Do you think he felt like doing what he did? When Andrew told us what had happened, we praised him, and he received a "Way to go, buddy! I'm so proud of you, and so is Jesus." But if he had simply done what he felt like doing, he would have just shut-up and gone with the program. Doing his daddy's will didn't feel good until he was in my presence and could hear my "well done," but he knew he was doing the right thing in spite of his feelings. The will of God can sometimes feel like deprivation.

Sometimes the Will of God Feels Exhausting

In the book of Hebrews, the author writes, "You have need of endurance, so that when you have done the will of God, you may receive what was promised" (10:36).

Why do we need endurance? Because doing the will of God is a hard grind at times. The will of God sometimes requires doing good for a long time with little or no reward, and that can become exhausting.

I am privileged to have a number of friends on the mission field. Each of these brave souls ministers in a foreign land with a foreign culture and language. They share the gospel of Christ which is a foreign idea. Progress often comes terribly slowly, and to Americans brought up with the idea of gauging themselves by their "results," this can be a hard experience. Inevitably their emotions begin to fray—even though they are clearly obeying the command of Christ. They are caused to throw themselves once again upon the only One who can uphold them and keep them going.

At times we need to remember Elijah the prophet who, after doing the will of God so boldly, was ready to die because his emotions had brought him to such a point of exhaustion. Everything God told him to do he had done. He had battled and defeated the false prophets of Baal, and vindicated God in the presence of all Israel. The outcome was a total success from all vantage points. But the result of his obedience was the wrath of evil Jezebel, whose prophets these were. She began to seek him out to kill him. At one point he just didn't think he could take it any longer and was in the depths of despair. Another word is *exhausted!*

Ministry, service, helping, can be exhausting. After a Sunday morning of preaching, teaching, greeting, and encouraging, I'm a basket case. Having expended huge amounts of emotional energy, I'm worthless for hours. Just ask my wife! In those moments I embody the Hallmark® card that my children got for me one year at Father's Day. It read, "A good dad like you is hard to find—but the couch is a good place to start." We all had a good laugh over that.

At a pastors' conference I once attended, Howard Hendricks, an internationally recognized Christian educator, leader, and author, once shared in a moment of transparency what would often happen when he was younger and went out of town to speak at conferences. There God would work mightily through him. But upon his return he would lapse into a state of depression that could last for days. Even when the results of our ministry are obvious and we can clearly see we have been in the direct will of God—we can feel exhausted.

Sometimes the Will of God Feels Humiliating

We are called by God to serve one another, and thus fulfill the law of Christ, and that is a position of humility. Someone once said, "No one minds being *called* a servant, until they start getting *treated* like one." People will abuse our service or fail to appreciate it, and that is humiliating. But the command to serve one another applies even when we don't feel like doing it. The disciples didn't feel like washing each other's feet, yet they knew Christ had called them to do it.

As we can see from these principles, the will of God can create a plethora of emotions in us as we contemplate it in all its various experiences. There is no one emotion we can feel that proves we are in the will of God. When we trust our feelings to lead us into the will of God, we are assigning them a task they weren't designed for. When this occurs there remains no clear parameters for discovering the leading of God other than how we feel about it at the moment. Thus, our feelings, our desires, our "gut reactions," become to us the will of God. The result is that we become gods unto ourselves, trusting in the reliability of our feelings.

"Feelings come and go," wrote C. S. Lewis, "and when they come a good use can be made of them: they cannot be our regular spiritual diet."[16]

The brutal truth is that very often the will of God is a steady determined walk right into the line of fire, where Satan will shoot emotional missiles designed to make you feel that God's will is the most dangerous and foolhardy task you could attempt. Erwin Lutzer puts it this way:

> Most Christians understand that salvation comes by faith, apart from feelings. But they think that the Spirit-controlled life requires some type of mystical experience—a feeling, a surge of power, or being overcome by waves of love. Those experiences are usually not around when you need them.[17]

More often than not my "gut feeling" has kept me from doing God's will. It has kept me from sharing my faith (I have chickened out a number of times), it has kept me from reaching out to someone in need *(Oh, they'll just misunderstand, or they'll get annoyed with me)*, it has kept me from warning a brother or sister of the danger of a sin they were dabbling in *(I'll jeopardize our friendship, or come across as judgmental)*.

On the other side, going with my gut feeling can cause me to give in to sexual temptation, can cause me to keep my mouth shut when I should speak for God, can cause me to buy something I can't afford, can cause me to take that second, third, fourth, and fifth drink, or can cause me to explode in violent anger. Time after time when someone has stumbled on one of these issues you will hear them say, "It just *felt* like the right thing to do."

SHOULD I IGNORE MY FEELINGS?

Well, then, what do we do with feelings? Do we ignore them? Years ago, I would have said yes. It was the commonly repeated mantra, "Ignore your feelings, they aren't reliable." But should we, or can we, ignore our feelings? Asking if we should try to ignore our feelings as we seek the will of God is a little like asking, "Could I have built my house without any wood?" The obvious answer is no, of course not. Wood is essential to the building, it is a major component of the building.

What we should ask is, "Can I build a house with wood alone?" Again the answer is no. I'll need hammers, and saws, and levels, and nails, and sandpaper, and other tools to make the wood useful and beautiful. I'll discover right off that some of the wood is simply unfit to use; it needs to be discarded. It is too unwieldy, warped, or damaged. Other pieces will need to be cut, or routed, or fitted, or sanded. And at the end, very little of the wood will be showing, since it will all be covered over with other materials.

Can I live my life and find God's direction by ignoring my feelings? No, no more than I could build my house without using wood.

But can I find the will of God for my life by depending upon my feelings alone? No; feelings, like the wood, have to be thoroughly examined, and some must be discarded right off. Other feelings will have to be leveled by advice, others need to be cut to fit God's Word, while others need to be molded by prayer. Because feelings, like wood, can be changed from one form into another in the process of discovering God's will for my life.

Feelings are a part of our decision-making process, and God will use them. God created us as emotional beings and while we cannot completely rely on feelings for direction, they must not be completely dismissed either. If Satan can seek to lead us through twisting our feelings, certainly God will use them as one of the means of leading us. I felt God leading me to minister in the church I co-pastor, marry my wife, and even to write this book. But feelings weren't my sole guide, they were only one of the factors I considered as I pondered God's will.

We must examine our feelings as we would examine wood for a house. We must have some way to measure our feelings against an improper conclusion. I believe we can benefit by considering the following questions regarding the role of emotions in understanding God's will.

Does This Feeling Contradict a Scriptural Principle or Truth?

God does not contradict Himself. He will never lead us by our feelings to do something He has expressly forbidden in His Word. If we feel "led" to do something we know is expressly forbidden in Scripture, we can know we have been hit by one of Satan's emotional missiles, designed to get us off the path of God's will. It is useless in discerning the true will of God.

Emotions often come in great waves, and if we understand this, we can prepare ourselves to remain stable through these periods. Spending much of my life in southern California, and near the beaches, I have always enjoyed body-surfing. While I am out in the water, waiting for the next perfect wave, other less-perfect waves roll over me, all fully capable of tumbling me head-over-heels to shore, filling my mouth and lungs with saltwater, my eyes with sand, and skinning up my knees on the sand and rocks. Each wave is capable of overwhelming me if I just stand still and let it hit me.

This is why experienced body surfers learn to swim toward a large wave that is preparing to crest, and then dive down toward its base, grabbing for the sand firmly with both hands, and letting the powerful wave roll over them. If you do this you will experience only a mild rocking of your body, rather than the violent thrashing the wave is capable of delivering.

Before you take your next big step, share your plans and reasoning with several well-seasoned and wise brothers or sisters in Christ. Let your feelings be subject to some other, perhaps more objective, opinions. The Bible tells us that in a multitude of counselors there is victory (Proverbs 11:14). I know a number of people who ignored this advice, and it ultimately led them to disaster. They only wish they had subjected their feelings to the counsel of others, and not ignored the advice they had been given.

Have I Honestly Examined My Motivations?

Our desires act as kindling to our feelings. If we have a secret desire to be rich, for example, that desire will ignite our emotions and make us susceptible to "get rich quick" schemes.

Occasionally I come across eager Christian entrepreneurs. They have a plan or objective (usually to make large sums of money). And based upon how excited they are about their goals, they prepare to launch out. But they forget about the Holy Spirit who convicts us of improper motivation (James 4:2–3).

So when the Holy Spirit begins His work on their hearts, they try to make a deal with Him. *Now* they want to make large sums of money *for the Lord!* After all, they reason, if they're millionaires, look how much money they could give to good Christian causes! It is only with great effort that I can keep a straight face during such conversations.

This has become an attempt to spiritualize sin. A sinful desire can't be sanctified, it must be confessed. If our motivation is really to be generous to Christian ministries, let us begin now, with what we have.

Is this thing I feel "led" to do really just stroking some ego need in me, or some vengeful or spiteful emotion in me, or some materialistic desire in me? Hard questions to ask, but important.

Is This Feeling Prompted by a Genuine Concern for Others?

I'll never forget the time I received a cruel and mean-spirited letter by someone in a church I was attending. The letter began with the words, "You may not appreciate these things I'm going to say now, but I'm saying them in love, and I hope later you will be able to see that." It is now over twenty-five years later, and I can honestly say I never saw love; neither did anyone else. He probably felt led to do this, but his leading was not prompted by a genuine concern for me; it was self-serving.

Has This Feeling Stood the Test of Time?

At times in the past I have made hasty decisions based on powerful feelings. Unfortunately, these feelings soon passed, but not the repercussions of my decision based on those feelings. I acted too quickly on my feelings. I have learned not to make major decisions based on how I feel at night, or in the middle of the night, but to see if I still feel the same in the light of day. The writer of Proverbs was aware of these waves of emotions: "*Do not be afraid of sudden fear*, nor of the onslaught of the wicked when it comes, for the Lord will be your confidence and will keep your foot from being caught" (Proverbs 3:25, emphasis added).

I have made it a habit to give time to all strong feelings that could result in significant decisions in my life, before acting on them. I have learned that emotions that feel so intensely strong one moment can all but disappear in another.

There was a time in my ministry I was so discouraged that I quit. The emotions igniting this decision were so overwhelming that I couldn't imagine ever wanting to be a pastor again. I was despondent, weary to the bone, and I couldn't generate even one positive emotion to keep me in pastoral ministry.

Fortunately, I didn't *actually* quit. My resignation was a mental one, an acknowledgment that I had been emotionally rolled and tossed and finally deposited on the beach of despair, unable to get up anymore. I didn't write out a resignation because I was aware of how fragile and therefore untrustworthy my emotions were at the moment. So for a while, ministry was a mechanical going-through-the-motions affair for me.

But later, when God reignited my desire for ministry stronger than ever, I was grateful I hadn't followed all the dictates of my emotions. I had to learn to ask myself, is this truly God's leading, or am I just reacting or panicking in some difficult time of life?

Am I Reading More into This Feeling Than I Should?

We must be wary of knee-jerk reactions to our emotions. One who feels a need to learn more about the Bible may decide he or she is called into vocational ministry. One who feels a strong pull toward music ministry may decide to sell the house, quit a job, and go full-time into Christian music ministry.

I have known people who have started businesses, sold homes, and changed jobs all because they "felt" it was the right thing to do. Later, their plans turned to disaster. They had not thought or prayed this issue out at any great length, and finally tiring of the struggle, just gave in to their emotions.

I once knew a college-age girl who told me she wanted to become a radio disc jockey—something she was not at all gifted for. In reality, what she desperately wanted was some attention and someone to talk to. She took her feeling and read into it more than she should have. It's easy to do.

Is My "Feeling" a Disguised Desire to Escape My Current Situation?

A troubled marriage, a problem relationship, a sense of failure in a career, discouragement, or setbacks are just a few of the "feelings" we can use to justify escaping a present situation. A feeling that is prompted by a desire to escape a current situation can easily be mistaken for God's leading.

All of these questions need to be asked of feelings we may have. C. S. Lewis once wrote, "Don't bother much about your feelings. When they are humble, loving, brave, give thanks for them; when they are conceited, selfish, cowardly, ask to have them altered. In neither case are they you, but only a thing that happens to you. What matters is your intentions and your behaviors."[18]

Perhaps this best sums it up for us. We are a people desperately in need of putting our feelings in their proper perspectives. We must recognize emotions for the strong impact they have on our lives, but never ever engage them as our sole guides.

You can act independently of, and yes, at times, even directly in spite of your feelings. Not only can you, but at times your ultimate joy and contentment will completely depend upon it.

Very few moments in our lives are more fulfilling than the ones in which we realize that we do not have to act at the beck and call of the powerful waves of emotions that have heretofore tossed us at will.

In the early days of the round-ups on the great western cattle ranches, cowboys would often take a particularly ornery wild horse and harness him to a little burro. The two would then be set free to roam the desert range. They would buck and kick and snort, and the little burro would be thrown around by that great steed like a rag doll. They would disappear over the horizon, that great wild steed dragging the poor hapless burro along with him.

They could be gone for days, but eventually they would come back. The scene would always be the same: the little burro would be seen first, trotting back across the horizon, leading the now submissive steed in tow.

Somewhere out in that range the great steed would spend its strength, like a great wave, and the little burro in that moment would take charge and become the master, leading them both safely back home with the right attitude.

Maybe you feel like that little burro must have when strong emotions attach themselves to you and threaten to take away the control of your life. We've all been there.

Just remember that like the great waves and the great steed, all emotions will eventually spend themselves. They are undeniably strong forces in our lives, but they're not very good guides. If we are going to realistically address the issue of discovering the will of God for our lives, we must first deal with the issue of our feelings.

While feelings are something many people rely on in the search for God's will, there is something else that almost equals it for popularity. Circumstances!

People who are making decisions often give more weight to circumstances than other factors they're considering. This is one of the areas in which I've seen the most profound disillusionment when things go sour. So, let's take a look.

FOLLOW THROUGH

1. If I were honest, I would have to say that subjective feelings have played a

   ❏ primary
   ❏ large
   ❏ secondary
   ❏ small

part in my search for the will of God. (Check one and explain why.)

2. The last time the will of God felt confusing to me was when

3. What one thing am I sure God wants me to do, but I'm afraid to do it?

4. The last time doing the will of God in my life felt great was when

5. We talked about a number of emotions that the will of God can produce in our lives. Can I think of some that weren't mentioned?

6. "When we trust our feelings to lead us into the will of God, we are assigning them a task they weren't designed for. When this occurs there remains no clear parameters for discovering the leading of God other than how we feel about it at the moment. Thus, our feelings, our desires, our 'gut reactions,' become to us the will of God." How do I respond to this statement?

7. How important have feelings been in the decisions I've made in my life?

8. Do I feel that I have been unbalanced by (1) leaning too heavily upon feelings, or (2) discarding them altogether? My basic personality leans toward . . . (choose either (1) or (2) and then explain why you did).

9. Whose counsel do I choose before I make major decisions? (What is the result?)

10. When was the last time I mistook a disguised need for God's leading?

11. The last time I made a decision based on overwhelming emotions was when

12. The most important thing I've learned today about feelings and the will of God is

Making Contact

Today, you are facing some decision, pondering some choice, or determining some direction you intend to take. As you've learned a little more about your emotional tendencies, you may want to find a greater balance. Knowing now that emotions can come in strong waves, ask God for greater discernment.

CHAPTER EIGHT

Circumstances: The Fool's Gold of Life

In the days of the California Gold Rush, miners came from all over the country to make their fortune. They were all looking for one thing: gold-colored rock, the shiny metal that would make them rich. Unfortunately, they weren't all experienced miners. Many of them did indeed find beautiful gold rock and were sure that they had struck it rich. Later, much to their chagrin, they learned that what they had struck was not gold, but pyrite, a gold look-alike, commonly called "fool's gold."

Pyrite is found everywhere, and it looks very much like gold. It has all the coloring, glitter, and shine of the real thing. Fortunately, there are ways to determine whether pyrite, the look-alike, is the real thing. One test is by heating both metals. Real gold can be heated on a hot stove without deteriorating, but fool's gold, pyrite, will sizzle, smoke, and smell horrible.

In the same way, many people who are aggressively pursuing the will of God for their lives can easily be misled by circumstantial look-alikes. More than one person has looked at circumstances in life the same way early miners looked at pyrite. While they were sure this was a sign of impending fortune, that they had hit "pay dirt," only too late did they realize it was only fool's gold.

After an agonizingly long search for the will of God, it is easy to misinterpret a special circumstance that might arise. In our excitement over the situation, we don't scrutinize these circumstances closely enough. Later, when the decisions we make begin to sizzle, smoke, and smell bad, like the pyrite, we feel God was derelict, or even deceitful, in His leading.

We need biblical principles for addressing the circumstances in our lives. If I am looking for a new job, and one comes along, does that circumstance indicate God's leading? That is, should I quit my present job to take the new one? If a woman is lonely, wanting to get married, and someone comes into her life, is this an answer to our prayer, or not? If a man is low on money, and someone comes along with a surefire plan to increase his bank account, is this circumstance the leading of God, or is it fool's gold?

How do we know if these circumstances are meant to lead us to take a certain action, or are to be ignored? In dealing with the issue of finding the will of God, we need to look at this issue closely. I have seen too many people build a case for a certain direction they took in life based on circumstances alone, and often the consequences were tragic, both situationally, and spiritually.

Nothing is worse than believing that you have followed the clear leading of God, only later to see everything you tried sizzle, smoke, and end up stinking to high heaven! But in spite of this we can take heart, because I believe the Bible does provide principles that can help us know how to approach circumstances wisely. So let's take a look at some.

Circumstances Alone Are Not Reliable Guides to God's Will

We get a fascinating insight into this issue by simply paying attention to Webster's definition of the word *circumstance*. *Circumstance* is defined as "a fact or event that must be considered along with another fact or event." Even in its definition we can see that circumstances must be viewed in light of other information. A circumstance may indeed provide an arrow pointing us in a certain direction, but unfortunately a circumstance can just as easily point us in the wrong direction.

Think of Jesus' disciples. Standing before thousands of people, Jesus turns to His disciples, and says, "Give them something to eat!" (Matthew 14:16). The crowds had followed Him, and they were hungry (vv. 16–21). He knew that. The disciples were no doubt sympathetic to His compassion, but come on! How could they have looked at the thousands of hungry people, and those five loaves of bread and two fishes, and determined what step to take? If they had relied on circumstances alone, would they ever have started passing out the little bit they had, or would they have sent everyone away?

Or, what of the apostles? If the apostles had relied on circumstances alone to determine their actions, would they have continued to preach the gospel, knowing full well it would invite trouble, persecution, even death? Would Shadrach, Meshach, and Abed-nego in the book of Daniel have been willing to enter the fiery furnace for not bowing down to the king's idol if they had based their decisions on circumstances alone? Would Noah have built the ark if he had relied only upon circumstances to give him direction—especially with all the ridicule he endured?

And think of Job and his friends. When Job was afflicted with terrible suffering, and his friends came over to try to comfort him, do you remember their immediate conclusion, on the basis of circumstances? They were sure Job had sinned and simply had not repented, and they didn't hesitate to tell him so. What else could these circumstances have meant? If you remember, those circumstances were manipulated by Satan. Job had done nothing wrong, and circumstances were not evidence of God's displeasure with him. In these cases, and many others, we can readily see that circumstances alone are not reliable guides to determining God's will for our lives.

Having said that, we must be quick to add that circumstances can, at times, be helpful.

Circumstances, Properly Balanced, Can Be Used To Discover God's Will

Because a circumstance can be defined as "a fact or event that must be considered along with another fact or event," we can say that after considering carefully the whole context of our given circumstances, we can certainly use them as part of our process of discovering God's will.

I remember how, when I was fresh out of seminary, finding the will of God for my ministry was paramount. The task also seemed terribly difficult. I felt led by God to start a church; I had for some time. I desperately wanted to be a church planter, but nothing seemed to materialize.

After a while I received an offer to candidate at a local small church, and by that time I was willing to take any position of ministry. I put church planting on the back burner, because I fervently wanted to be in ministry. This seemed like a very positive circumstance, an "open door" as we often say. I figured that this was where God was leading me, on the basis of this circumstance. I had a number of misgivings about the situation, but I ignored them in light of this positive circumstance that just seemed to scream, "Go this way."

In the meantime, as I waited several months to hear from this church, I heard that my denomination was interested in starting a church in Rancho Santa Margarita, California, a brand-new community not far from where I lived. When I heard that, it rekindled my original dream of starting a church. Now I had a conflict of circumstances. One circumstance seemed to say, "Go this way," and another circumstance seemed to say, "No, go this way!" Isn't that the way it often is? Have you ever been there? Maybe you are there now.

Circumstances alone couldn't provide positive direction. So I prayed and took stock of my personality, the gifts God had given me, my passion for church planting, and the very different demands of pastoring an older church in decline. I also considered the fact that the denomination was seeking someone just like me to work in Rancho Santa Margarita. I eventually made the decision to start the church, a decision I never regretted and saw God bless greatly.

Over the years I have learned more about my personality and God-given design, and I am repeatedly reminded that my decision was born of God. I realize that I am attracted and motivated to begin new things. Distinctly different demands are placed on someone trying to revive a church in decline, as opposed to the demands placed on a church planter. Neither undertaking is easy, or more spiritual—but they are definitely different.

God used circumstances in my decision, but my decision was not based on circumstances alone. I had to balance different circumstances to arrive at His clear leading in my life. But there is another principle to consider that will help us learn to govern circumstances, and not have circumstances govern us.

God's Word Always Overrules Conflicting Circumstances

Sometimes in our desire for a certain thing to be God's will, we are tempted to exaggerate the meaning of circumstances. We so strongly want to be confirmed in our current direction that we read circumstances like tea leaves. What often results is that we are governed more by circumstances than by the clear teaching of God's Word.

For example, take the scenario so often occurring today. A spouse is in a Christian marriage, but it isn't satisfying. Because of breakdowns in communication, loneliness and unhappiness deepen in the relationship. So one or the other innocently seeks someone to ease the loneliness. Then at work, or at the club, or in the neighborhood, someone becomes attentive at just the right time, the time of emotional and spiritual poverty. Soon, a harmless relationship begins, and it takes away some of the loneliness. But before long, this stranger becomes the object of affection. When confronted by this sin, this person will frequently respond, "How can you deny that this is the will of God? It has filled such a need in my life. God must have brought this person into my life, this relationship has to be God's will for me."

Was this real gold, or fool's gold? Fool's gold! How can we know this? Because 1 Thessalonians 4:3 says, "This is the will of God, your sanctification; that is, that you abstain from sexual immorality." Exodus 20:14 reminds us "You shall not commit adultery." Over and over in Scripture, from the Old Testament to the New, we read God's command that we abstain from immorality of every kind. A very clear biblical principle would have put that circumstance in perspective. It was unfortunately an unused tool. When we've already decided what we want, we will always be able to find some way to justify our actions, but to do so often requires reading more into circumstances than we should.

When a circumstance seems to be leading you to do something the Bible, or biblical principles clearly prohibit, that circumstance must be ignored. And this leads naturally to our next governing principle.

Circumstances That Seem Negative Don't Always Mean "Stop," and Circumstances That Seem Positive Don't Always Mean "Go"

In the books of Ezra and Nehemiah we read the story of the Jews leaving their exile in Persia and returning home to Jerusalem to rebuild the temple. God had miraculously moved in the heart of a secular ruler named Cyrus not only to allow them to return to their own lands, but to fund the expedition, providing the resources they would need to do the rebuilding. This was an amazing answer to prayer. So the people returned to rebuild, fired up with the knowledge that God had miraculously manipulated circumstances to allow them to return to their own land.

But as soon as they returned, they encountered hostile resistance. In Nehemiah 4:7–9, we read about the situation.

> Now when Sanballat, Tobiah, the Arabs, the Ammonites, and the Ashdodites heard that the repair of the walls of Jerusalem went on, and that the breaches began to be closed, they were very angry. And all of them conspired together to come and fight against Jerusalem and to cause a disturbance in it. But we prayed to our God, and because of them we set up a guard against them day and night.

God had opened virtually every door for them to return home, but now the very work they had been sent to do seemed cursed. Instead of all the circumstances working out just like they had expected, they were all negative. What did the Jews under Nehemiah do?

> When I saw their fear, I rose and spoke to the nobles, the officials, and the rest of the people: "Do not be afraid of them; remember the Lord who is great and awesome, and fight for your brothers, your sons, your daughters, your wives, and your houses."
>
> When our enemies heard that it was known to us, and that God had frustrated their plan, then all of us returned to the wall, each one to his work. From that day on, half of my servants carried on the work while half of them held the spears, the shields, the bows, and the breastplates; and the captains were behind the whole house of Judah. Those who were rebuilding the wall and those who carried burdens took their load with one hand doing the work and the other holding a weapon. As for the builders, each wore his sword girded at his side as he built, while the trumpeter stood near me (Nehemiah 4:14–18).

Isn't that great? They didn't let circumstances dictate their actions. They knew they had been called of God to rebuild, and opposition or not, they were going to keep going. While they worked, one hand held a tool, and the other a weapon. This was a healthy response to negative circumstances. God wasn't saying through circumstances, "Stop the work," He was saying, "Continue, and I will deal with the opposition." I see too many Christians today allowing negative circumstances to keep them from doing the clear will of God. The circumstances they point to become for them divine "permission to be absent" slips.

When we do the things God has called us to do, we will sometimes encounter severe and hostile circumstances. Sharing our faith, taking a stand against moral evil, defending biblical truth, and proclaiming Jesus as the only way to salvation are just a few examples, among many. The Bible makes it clear that all those who desire to live godly lives in Christ Jesus will be persecuted (2 Timothy 3:12). This means we should expect to have to act in the face of negative circumstances at times. The Bible is replete with such examples. We must not let negative circumstances determine our actions when we know God has commanded us to do something.

In the Old Testament we read of King Saul becoming increasingly jealous of David's rising popularity among the people (1 Samuel 18:1–11). His victory over Goliath and the Philistines made him popular among the people; unfortunately, more popular than Saul. This aroused the king to seek David's death. Time after time Saul went in search of David to kill him, and several times divine circumstances thwarted him.

As Saul was trying to kill David, David was "circumstantially" given several opportunities to kill Saul instead, and his men even urged him to do it (1 Samuel 24). But he refused, and that was his legacy. Even Saul was ashamed of himself when he realized the integrity that David had exercised by not killing him when he had the chance. Circumstances and opportunity alone did not dictate his actions. We see this further in the next principle:

Circumstances Should Not Rule Our Lives

It was one of paganism's attributes that its followers were captive to the whims of circumstance, seeing in them the pleasure or displeasure of the gods. We, as Christians, are not at the whim of circumstances; we have been given wisdom, God's Word, prayer, and His Spirit in us to give us discernment.

I remember a time when I felt at the whim of circumstances. I'm not sure where or how I developed this crazy notion, but I had come to believe early in life that if everything started going my way, I was in some state of blessedness, or "luck." In those moments I felt like I had the Midas touch: anything I tried would succeed. On the other hand, if everything seemed to be going wrong, I would not attempt anything significant, because I was sure it would fail.

It was so bad that I would try to wait for a "good day" before I would attempt anything significant. I would not ask a girl out if circumstances had not been favorable that day. There was no reason to, she was sure to say no. I know that sounds crazy, but I actually lived several years with that kind of mind-set.

Then one day, talking to an older Christian brother, I mentioned my modus operandi, and he turned to me and said with astonishment, "Why Dan, that's superstition!" As strange as it seems now, that was the first time I had ever recognized it as such. I was a captive to circumstances. I might as well have been consulting a crystal ball or my horoscope for direction in life.

Once I realized I was being ruled by circumstances I took a great step. I had wanted to ask this particular girl out, but lately all circumstances had been bad, things weren't going my way at all. One of the hardest things I ever did was call that girl up and ask her out, in the midst of all the negative circumstances I was encountering. But when I asked her out, she not only said, "Yes," she was excited I had asked, and had been hoping I would. I learned an important lesson that day. Circumstances can't be trusted, they aren't the will of God, they are merely facts or events that must be considered along with other facts, events, and truths.

Are you captive to circumstances like I was? Are you allowing circumstances to make all your decisions for you, ruling your life? You need freedom, freedom found in the truth. Circumstances are not the will of God, and they can't be trusted alone for guidance.

Some Circumstances Need to Be Faced Down

We need to become aware of the strategy of Satan in our lives. Some circumstances we will encounter in life have been produced and manipulated by Satan to get us to change our course, and move away from God's clear will for our lives. He is not known as "the tempter" for nothing (Matthew 4:3; 1 Thessalonians 3:5).

Did Satan have a hand in creating the circumstance of a beautiful naked Bathsheba bathing at just the precise moment King David was walking along his palace walls (2 Samuel 11)? This was a circumstance that David needed to face down. He needed to look away and tell himself, "It doesn't matter how beautiful that woman is, or how lonely I feel, or how available she seems to me as the king. She's *not* available to me, God has said that clearly in Scripture." He needed to face down this circumstance, but he didn't. He allowed the circumstance to dictate his actions.

If the early Christians had considered the circumstances of certain persecution to be absolute signs that they weren't to preach the gospel, none of us would be followers of Christ today. The fact of persecution had to be considered, to be sure, but along with it other things had to be taken into account. Those things included the resurrection of Christ, the Great Commission Christ had given them to "make disciples" of all the nations, and the fact that their lives would not end at death, but God Himself would usher them into His eternal presence, and their heavenly reward.

Persecution was not a circumstance that indicated God didn't want them to share the gospel, it was simply a circumstance that highlighted the price their obedience would exact from them. In effect, this was a circumstance that had to be faced down!

Prayer Is Key

So, just what approach should we take to circumstances when we are seeking the will of God?

While I am going to share what I think is a biblically sound, wise course of action, I need to preface it by putting prayer in its proper place. Above and beyond everything we have said so far, we need to be continually mindful that this is God's will we are seeking. Before, during, and after every point suggested here, comes prayer.

Not a perfunctory "Lord, show me Your will" prayer, which some imagine is the magic key to unlock divine blessing. Persistent, honest, and vulnerable prayer is required—prayer that comes from a heart that is willing to accept whatever answer will come. Prayer that acknowledges the perfection of His will for us, and His eagerness to share it with us.

The more emotionally tied we are to a certain hoped-for conclusion, the more we need to bathe our decisions and thoughts in prayer, so we can exercise wise judgment in circumstances.

How then, do we approach circumstances? Let's look at John for a moment, and walk with him through a very important decision in his life. John has always been fairly musical, and recently while visiting a music store, something he always feels drawn to do, he looks at some of the music that is being sold. His wife Betty is standing by him, and he turns to her and says, "Man, I can write better music than this." Betty has heard this before and has noticed that John never does anything about it, so she's ready with a new response: "Okay, John, if you can do better, why don't you?"

John smiles. It's a secret desire he has harbored for a while, but suddenly it's something he's got to try. "Okay, I will." John is now filled with a new resolve. He feels that this was an important moment in his life, that somehow he has found something that would be very fulfilling, maybe even something God is calling him to do. This conversation with Betty has sparked a fire in him to begin to write music, with the hope that one day, someone will be selling his music at the store.

How is John to approach this circumstance, and others that will come his way? First, he will need to understand the first principle of this chapter: Circumstances alone are not reliable guides to God's will.

Remember our definition of a circumstance: a fact or event that must be considered along with another fact or event. If John wants to approach this circumstance wisely, he needs to face the fact that this circumstance might be just that, one event to be considered along with other events and facts. He's seeking God's will, but circumstantially he has to realize he hasn't arrived yet. This is only one piece in the puzzle, and he can't be sure yet just where it fits into God's will for his life.

He knows that direction in life often begins with a desire, but he also knows that desire alone isn't an indication of the direction God wants him to take. For him to act wisely, and biblically, he needs to apply the next principle.

Consider Other Significant Factors

Now this is risky for John because it might imperil his dream. John *wants* to seek God's will, but he also really *wants* to be a songwriter. He's not sure if he's ready to face the fact that his desire may not be God's will for his life, so this is a difficult moment for him. But if he is serious about seeking God's will, and using biblical principles of wisdom, he will begin to consider several significant factors in his life, including:

Desires

God is not interested in making sure we are miserable in our pursuits. He frequently works through our desires. The Bible tells us that God is interested in fulfilling our desires, but only when our way has been fully committed to Him.

> Delight yourself in the LORD; and He will give you the desires of your heart. Commit your way to the LORD, trust also in Him, and He will do it (Psalm 37:4–5).

John wants to be a songwriter, and the desire is growing stronger and stronger. He longs to write music that would glorify God and move His people to worship Him. This desire must not be ignored; it could be a very important consideration, yet he realizes that God's will is not always found through our desires. Our desires come from many different sources, including our sinful nature which encourages sinful pride and ego.

So, while John must start here, this is too often where people stop. John knows that his desires can change; what he wants today may not be what he wants tomorrow. He also knows that you can want the right thing for the wrong reason. So he decides that while he can't deny the desire, he will consider other important factors, too.

Godly Advice

While this aspect of seeking God's will has been stressed before, it cannot be overemphasized. There are others who know John's strengths and weaknesses, and they see them more objectively. They have a different point of view, another way of looking at John and the issue, maybe some practical experience they could share that would provide light on songwriting John had never previously considered. The reality of what we are seeking is often less fulfilling than the dreams we harbored of it. John knows he needs to be careful not to over-romanticize this new pursuit.

So John starts to broach the subject with some friends and musicians he knows, telling them of his desire to write songs, asking for their input. Many of them recognize that John is a gifted musician, and they know his love for music, so they encourage him to give it a try. So far so good. John moves ahead.

God-given Design

One of the most painful things we can do is to be honest about our abilities and strengths, our divine design. For example, someone who wants to be a movie star may have absolutely no aptitude for the job, but is attracted to the vocation because of the perks it affords. They want to be famous, rich, and important. They see successful actors or actresses as famous, rich, and important, hence their "calling" to be an actor.

John is reluctant to address this issue, because if he comes to the wrong conclusion, it can spell doom for his desire, and dreams die hard. But he musters up his courage and begins to assess his God-given design. He is a gifted musician, he knows that. Yet, while others have confirmed his abilities, he realizes that many people have received similar compliments and yet they weren't skilled enough to write Christian songs that a publisher would consider.

As he begins to evaluate his skills, he realizes that his strength is in composing, and his weakness is in performance. It's not that John isn't a gifted singer; he is. But, he realizes honestly, that many others are more gifted performers. No, he realizes with some joy that his interest and skill seem to be in creating melodies. He remembers back to his high school days when he wrote several songs for the choir and his compositions were well-received. When he listens to music he is drawn not to the people singing the songs but to the way the notes are arranged. This is what fascinates him.

John has come to a wise conclusion. He is more gifted for writing music than performing it. The idea of performing the songs he writes does not particularly appeal to him, but the idea of writing songs for others does. John remembers several people in his past who suggested he try his hand at writing music because they saw a real aptitude there. Armed with this, John considers another factor.

Responsibilities

John stops to consider something very important. He is not young and single and free of family-related responsibilities. He is married, with a growing family. He is a husband, father, and employee of a computer firm.

It is tempting for John to just decide to take all his free time to begin writing music, but his wife needs his free time too. And he has a son and two daughters who want to spend time with him. He needs to consider his current commitments and the time it will take for him to be successful as he thinks about starting to write songs. This leads to the next factor to consider.

Level of Involvement

This is something John had not really considered before, but he now realizes is crucial. Is this desire to be a songwriter a leading into a new vocation or a sidelight venture? Is songwriting something he should consider as a future full-time, part-time, or free-time calling?

Will this desire fulfill the need everyone has for a healthy diversion from the demands of his regular vocation, or will it one day become his vocation? This is an important question to ask at the beginning: Is God leading me to full-time songwriting, or does He want me to do this with a portion of my free time?

John has seen a number of people make great mistakes by selling their houses, quitting their jobs, and putting all their time and energy into something in the belief that God was calling them to do this full-time. He has seen too many of these ventures fail miserably and the disappointment these people then felt with God. He didn't want to make this mistake.

He asked himself some hard questions and finally realized that for now, at least, he would just seek to fulfill a desire, not a new vocation. While God may lead him to something else sometime in the future, he had to admit that he is very happy being a computer programmer. His involvement would be to keep songwriting at the hobby level. He would approach it seriously and professionally, but simply keep a watch on the amount of time he devoted to it.

This led him to the final factor to consider.

Timing

John was eager to begin, but wisely he decided to stop for a moment and consider whether he had the time right now to start this new pursuit. He was still attending some additional classes for his computer programming job, and the kids' soccer and basketball games would tie up his weekends for at least another three months.

It was tempting to drop out of the computer class, but he remembered that he had decided that songwriting wasn't going to be a vocational pursuit, so his decision was made easier. He decided to finish the class and become a better computer programmer. He would also wait until the kids' games were over, and he could talk with Betty about scheduling in the free time he would need to write songs.

This appealed to Betty, because she didn't have to worry that John was going to quit his job, abandon their livelihood, and live on "hopes and dreams." She loved John and wanted him to pursue his God-given talents. They sat down and were able to determine a schedule when John could begin to write songs, and she could help him by scheduling around these. Enough time was given to keeping their marriage relationship alive and well, and family time sacred, so that they could both be excited about John's songwriting ambitions.

With these factors weighed, John was now going to have to do something even more difficult, found in our next principle.

Guard Against Premature Emotional Commitment

John's excitement about writing songs was intensifying rapidly. Try as he might he couldn't help but begin to picture himself writing songs and having them sung by Christian artists.

When a circumstance seems to point to something we have wanted desperately for a long time it's easy to "move ourselves right in." We can begin to see this prematurely as a "sure thing." John began to daydream at work about what it would be like to have his songs published. Then reality caught hold. He hadn't written a single song, or even tried. He wasn't going to be able to try for several months. While this was discouraging for a few days, it gave him a renewed awareness of how powerfully emotions can push us to do things that wisdom might be restraining us from.

He remembered the Scripture verse he had memorized years ago: "Watch over your heart with all diligence, for from it flow the springs of life" (Proverbs 4:23). He saw how important it was to guard his heart from running too fast down a path he wasn't even sure was in God's will for him. If he didn't, he could end up being heartbroken, and blame God, and he didn't want to make that mistake. So he decided that he would follow the last principle.

Be Willing to Live with the Consequences of Your Final Decision

John realized that while everything seemed to be getting a green light, it was entirely possible, as remote as it now seemed, that this was not God's will for him. He could be mistaken. He might write songs that no one wanted, and become thoroughly disappointed and frustrated.

After he had gone through all the steps, he still had no guarantee that what he wanted was going to occur. The circumstance of Betty's challenge united with his desire might have been for another purpose. It was entirely possible that God wanted him to learn some valuable lessons in failure, or that there were lessons God wanted to teach him in this process that had little to do with his success at songwriting.

It could have been the prompting of God that led him to this quest to write songs, but it could also have been a hidden ego-need, or some other less-than-honorable motivation. Money was tight, and he wasn't sure that desire for more income wasn't part of his motivation. He realized he couldn't figure it all out, so he decided beforehand that he was willing to take the risk and live with the consequences of his final choice.

John decided that he would not hold God responsible for a decision he was making. He decided at the outset that his dream might never pan out. This could be a long mining trip from which he would discover only pyrite, but he decided he would rather live with failure attempting something he really wanted, than with regret for never having tried.

The story of John is true, but the names and situations have been changed. I am John, and I didn't want to be a songwriter, but a book writer. During the process of getting my first book published I encountered many significant successes, and many daunting failures. I also dealt with all these issues I am sharing with you. Many positive circumstances that seemed to scream "You've done it!" later fizzled, and they stunk like pyrite. There were some serious disappointments, as several times I misunderstood circumstances.

Six years after I began, however, I published my first book. More importantly, I learned the difference between pyrite and gold, circumstances and the will of God. I urge you to seriously consider these steps if you are contemplating a move that would have major consequences in your life. The principles governing circumstances are safeguards that will help you throw away the pyrite and keep the gold in your own experiences.

But the experiences that I had with failure and success in writing bring up a whole new issue in the search for the will of God, and that is determining the difference between success and failure and the will of God.

These three issues can become problematic if not clearly understood. So, let's take a look.

FOLLOW THROUGH

1. In my search for the will of God, do I think I have mined more pyrite, or the real thing?

2. Why can't circumstances alone be a reliable guide to discovering God's will for my life?

3. The last time I relied too heavily on circumstances to determine God's will, the result was

4. Can I think of a time when the clear teaching of Scripture helped me truly assess the meaning of a circumstance (i.e., I was able to tell this circumstance was fool's gold, and not God's leading)?

5. The last time I continued on with something I felt was God's will for me, even though circumstances seemed negative was when

6. The last time I stopped doing something I felt was not God's will for me, even though the circumstances seemed positive was when

7. "Circumstances have ruled my life too many times." On a scale of 1–10 (1 being always ruled, 10 being never ruled), I rate myself about a _____. (Fill in and explain.)

8. A circumstance in life I wish I had faced down, but didn't was

9. A current circumstance that I feel I might need to face down is

10. Do I believe Satan can manipulate circumstances to lead me away from God's will? (Why or why not?)

11. The last time God used circumstances to lead me into His will was when

    The way I knew that was

Making Contact

As you look at different circumstances in your life right now, you need to learn how to approach them wisely. Reread Nehemiah 4:14–23 and commit yourself to facing down the circumstances you are convinced God has called you to face down, and putting the others through a "wisdom" grid (found in the story of John, the aspiring songwriter). Commit to memory Proverbs 4:23: "Watch over your heart with all diligence, for from it flow the springs of life."

CHAPTER NINE

Success, Failure, and the Will of God

John and Lynn want to have a baby, but they have been unable to, in ten years of marriage. However, everything else that could possibly go right has. John has a great job that he loves, they have a great marriage, good friends, and they get to enjoy many luxuries that others can't afford. But having a baby is their greatest desire, and they can't imagine ever being completely happy without children of their own. Lynn agonizes when she sees other mothers holding their babies, and this grief is taking more and more of a toll on her. Should they go to a fertility clinic? Should they adopt a child? John and Lynn want to know God's will in the matter, so they ask God which direction they should take.

Sally is a college student who is thinking about accepting Bob's proposal of marriage. She loves him very much, but she's concerned. She has had several difficult relationships with men in the past and doesn't want to make a mistake. She doesn't want her marriage to repeat the pattern of her two previous relationships, so she asks God to reveal whether Bob will be the one she has been looking for, the one who will be able to make her truly happy.

Ted is a grandfather nearing retirement age. He started a business when he was young, and he has built it into a strong company, with great potential for the future. His three sons have been involved with him in the business, and each one wants to head the company when Dad retires. Ted is concerned. Which one would run it most efficiently, and keep intact everything he has worked for all these years? Ted prays and asks God to reveal which son to put in charge to ensure the success of the company.

In each scenario, personal happiness was the ultimate goal. John and Lynn want a baby to make them happy, Sally wants a guarantee of a problem-free marriage to assure her happiness, and Ted wants to make sure that everything he has worked for so long remains strong as a legacy to himself.

One of the things that often drives our search for the will of God is our belief that if we find it, our venture will be successful—that we will live "happily ever after."

In this scenario, the will of God becomes to us a sort of talisman, a good luck charm, a guarantee of success. The result is, of course, that God Himself becomes a sort of talisman to us. The unstated assumption is that God would never intentionally lead me into failure, or pain, or loss. Those kinds of things couldn't be His will, we tell ourselves; those are punishments for misbehavior.

This brings us to a very important question: Is the will of God success? It is instructive to listen to Webster's definition of the word *succeed*; it means "to obtain a desired object or end." This is our world's definition of success. When the key to success is simply gaining what we desire, and we believe the will of God is for us to always be successful, then the only time we can be in the will of God is when we get what we want.

The truth is that we often seek to know the will of God about a decision we are making with the belief that in doing so we can insure ourselves against anything going wrong. If something does not go the way we want, we can immediately believe it is because we are out of His will. But is this the case?

The Bible clearly teaches that there are times when the perfect will of God for our lives is what we would label misfortune, failure, loss, or persecution.

Misfortune

Think of Joseph, who was sold into slavery by his own brothers, and left to die. Then, after that bit of luck, he is wrongfully accused of attempted rape and thrown into prison. In prison he helps several of the Pharaoh's trusted advisors, with their promise to remember him upon their release. They forgot! So Joseph spends several more years in prison. (Read Genesis 45:1–8.)

And yet, this was precisely what God intended for Joseph. It seems hard to accept, until we look at the situation from Joseph's perspective later. We read in Genesis 45:5–8:

> "Do not be grieved or angry with yourselves, because you sold me here, for God sent me before you to preserve life. For the famine has been in the land these two years, and there are still five years in which there will be neither plowing nor harvesting. God sent me before you to preserve for you a remnant in the earth, and to keep you alive by a great deliverance. Now, therefore, it was not you who sent me here, but God; and He has made me a father to Pharaoh and lord of all his household and ruler over all the land of Egypt."

We can understand how easily Joseph could have become bitter toward God for the terrible misfortune that had befallen him. But he didn't, and it is a stirring testimony to his conviction that God was in control of all that occurred—that He was working for a good purpose, not an evil one.

Failure

There are times when we try something that we are sure is within the will of God for us, yet failure, not success, is the result. We are like the disciples in Matthew 17, when they came upon a similar situation. Read along.

> When they came to the crowd, a man came up to Jesus, falling on his knees before Him, and saying, "Lord, have mercy on my son, for he is a lunatic, and is very ill; for he often falls into the fire, and often into the water. And I brought him to Your disciples, and they could not cure him." And Jesus answered and said, "O unbelieving and perverted generation, how long shall I be

with you? How long shall I put up with you? Bring him here to Me." And Jesus rebuked him, and the demon came out of him, and the boy was cured at once.

Then the disciples came to Jesus privately and said, "Why could we not drive it out?" And He said to them, "Because of the littleness of your faith; for truly I say to you, if you have faith the size of a mustard seed, you will say to this mountain, 'Move from here to there,' and it will move; and nothing shall be impossible to you.

["But this kind does not go out except by prayer and fasting"] (Matthew 17:14–21).

Until that moment, everything had been easy and automatic. But this time the disciples failed! Embarrassment and humiliation must have been written all over their faces as the crowd approached Jesus. But there was a lesson to be learned that success could not teach them; failure was a better instructor. And there are times in life when failure is simply a better instructor than success.

Loss

In the book of Hebrews, the author relates how many of Christ's followers have experienced loss.

Remember the former days, when, after being enlightened, you endured a great conflict of sufferings, partly by being made a public spectacle through reproaches and tribulations, and partly by becoming sharers with those who were so treated. For you showed sympathy to the prisoners and accepted joyfully the seizure of your property, knowing that you have for yourselves a better possession and a lasting one (Hebrews 10:32–34).

Isn't this fascinating? If we lost all our valuable property and were left with nothing but the shirts on our backs, we'd consider it a terribly tragic situation, wouldn't we? Yet, these folks experienced just that, and it didn't crush them at all. In fact, they accepted the situation joyfully! They knew something about the will of God that we haven't caught on to yet. They lost everything, but they considered it perfectly within the will of God, and so did the Lord. What a testimony that must have had!

Persecution

When Paul was imprisoned, he praised God because he had gotten an opportunity to share the gospel with many in Caesar's household. The perfect will of God was for him to go to prison and share Christ with those people. How else could he have gotten the opportunity? What ultimate impact might this have had on powerful people in the Roman government? (Philippians 1:12–14).

Sometimes what we need more than anything else is not to achieve what we want to achieve, not to catch what we're chasing, not to possess that which we have wanted all our lives.

WHEN FAILURE BECOMES SUCCESS

Human failure is often God's success; yet that is such a difficult concept to grasp. A beautiful example of this is found in the experience of Joseph Ton. Joseph Ton was a pastor of a church in Oradea, Romania, until he was exiled by the communist government in 1981. He wrote in an article later,

> Years ago I ran away from my country to study theology at Oxford. In 1972, when I was ready to go back to Romania, I discussed my plans with some fellow students. They pointed out that I might be arrested at the border. One student asked, "Joseph, what chances do you have of successfully implementing your plans?" I asked God this same thing, and God brought to my mind Matthew 10:16 "I send you out as sheep in the midst of wolves"—and seemed to say, "Tell me, what chance does a sheep surrounded by wolves have of surviving five minutes, let alone of converting the wolves? Joseph, that's how I send you: totally defenseless and without a reasonable hope of success. If

you are willing to go like that, go. If you are not willing to be in that position, don't go."

After our return, as I preached uninhibitedly, harassment and arrests came. One day during interrogation an officer threatened to kill me. Then I said, "Sir, your supreme weapon is killing. My supreme weapon is dying. Sir, you know my sermons are all over the country on tapes now. If you kill me, I will be sprinkling them with my blood. Whoever listens to them after that will say, 'I had better listen. This man sealed them with his blood.' So go ahead and kill me. I win the supreme victory then."[19]

The officer sent him home. "That gave me pause," Joseph said. "For years I was a Christian who was cautious because I wanted to survive. I had accepted all the restrictions the authorities put on me because I wanted to live. Now that I wanted to die, they wouldn't oblige. Now I could do whatever I wanted in Romania. For years I wanted to save my life, and I was losing it. Now that I wanted to lose it, I was winning it."

If we are seeking the will of God as a talisman to protect us from all evil and misfortune, and to guide us away from trouble and loss, we will be sadly disappointed, and angry, because that's not what God has in mind.

The will of God is to conform us into the image of Christ. "For those whom He foreknew, He also predestined to become conformed to the image of His Son" (Romans 8:29).

One of the things I believe causes such intense disappointment in this whole subject of seeking the will of God is our tendency to get detoured into the "results" will of God, rather than the "process" or "journey" will of God. Now these aren't magic words, but descriptive words that convey an understanding that is often missing.

We tend to look at life as a ladder that we climb, and with each rung we imagine ourselves edging nearer and nearer His perfect will for us. The first rung was when we accepted Christ, this we know. But after that, the purpose and identity of the rungs gets a little fuzzy.

Marriage certainly seems to be a rung for many of us, as are the births of our children.

We may see one rung as graduation, another as entering the vocation we feel He has "led" us into. Reaching these rungs is how we tend to measure our proximity to the perfect will of God. This can be measured in a variety of different ways.

- After years of preparation, finally entering our chosen vocation
- After years of loneliness, finally getting married
- Finally reaching a certain income level, or position of responsibility

When we reach this rung, whatever we perceive it to be, we are convinced that we are at or very near the will of God for our lives. But what happens when, after reaching that rung, the rung breaks, or is removed?

- We have to leave the mission field
- We lose our spouse to death or divorce
- We lose the job, lose the house, lose the status
- We get close, but never achieve our dreams

This is the problem with the ladder-rung perception of God's will: it is too results-oriented. Scripture doesn't say that God's will for Dan Schaeffer is to be a "successful" pastor all my life. And it's a good thing, because there are moments when *success* is the last word I would use to describe my pastoring.

It also doesn't say it's God's will that I get to live with my wife and children in health and happiness until I die peacefully in my sleep at age ninety-six. I may not make it to my next birthday! The effects of sin on this world are not suspended for me the moment I receive Christ. I have no special immunity to calamity or catastrophe or disappointment. My eternal destiny is forever and unalterably secured, and I have peace with God and a loving relationship with Him forever, but I will still get sick someday and die, and so will Annette and my children.

Calamity will strike the Schaeffer household just as surely as it will my non-believing neighbors. Some of my fondest dreams and ambitions will never be realized, all of which brings one back to consider the problem of the ladder-rung perception of the will of God.

CONFORMING TO THE WILL OF GOD

God has made it abundantly clear what His will is for me in the time I have left on earth, and for you too! It is not a mystery, and we don't have to search desperately to find it. His will is that you be conformed to the image of His Son! As Paul said so eloquently in Philippians, it was his deepest desire to "know Him and the power of His resurrection and the fellowship of His sufferings, being conformed to His death" (3:10).

We're eager to be conformed to His life, but what about His death?

It is so simple that we miss its importance. We are results-oriented and He is process-oriented. We seek destination, He seeks transformation—*a journey*.

> Do not be conformed to this world, but be transformed by the renewing of your mind, so that you may prove what the will of God is, that which is good and acceptable and perfect (Romans 12:2).

As a result, that one thing we wanted so badly we could taste it, so badly that we were sure it had to be the will of God for us, so badly that we have all our happiness tied up in its coming to pass, may simply not occur. Why? Because *getting* it wasn't part of God's program to conform us to the image of Christ. In fact, *not getting* what we most desire is often the single most transforming event in our entire lives.

I want to be serious here, because what I'm going to say is difficult, especially for those who are already bleeding internally from some wound of disappointment in seeking God's will.

You wanted health, but you got cancer!

You wanted a long, happy marriage—but your spouse tragically died.

You wanted a happy, two-parent home, but got a divorce and the struggle of being a single parent instead.

You invested years and years preparing for Christian ministry, sacrificing and working long hours, and now your opportunities have been taken away, and you feel you have no purpose left to your life.

Your child has walked away from the Lord and everything you stand for.

You've lost a child to death.

You are unable to have children of your own, and you're unable to adopt.

Your spouse has lost his or her faith, and become hostile to yours.

You've lost your business, your home, and your previous standard of living.

If what you dreamed for, hoped for, prayed for, planned for, and worked for goes up in smoke, and you've held to a belief in the ladder-rung will of God—misery, disappointment, resentment, and a feeling of "free-falling" out of God's will and favor will be your constant companions. You have invested all your happiness into a results- or destination-oriented perception of God's will. What now?

THE PROCESS BEFORE THE PRODUCT

I beg of you, for your sake, and truth's sake, to reconsider. God is conforming you into the image of Christ, something that even in your anger and despair you must agree you want. But often the happiness and contentment in our Christian life is so tangled up with some desire or ambition being realized that when God in His sovereign wisdom withholds it, it is a deeply painful moment.

We step back and scream, "Why did You waste my time, lead me on, mislead me!?" But He didn't. We have to accept that it simply may never have been part of His plan for us.

He was conforming us through the *process* of life, the process of preparing us to be a pastor or missionary, of trying to have a child, of coping with death, of dealing with the results of destructive behavior, so that we might learn to honor Him, and seek His will above all else in our lives.

Remember that the disciples had experienced almost unlimited success for three years walking with their Master. They cast out demons, healed the lame, were close to the most popular Man in the country, and near the end of His three years with them were so full of themselves they couldn't bear the thought of washing one another's feet. Surely they thought the kingdom of God had come, and they would sit and rule with Christ, with honor and authority. It was just a matter of time, they must have told themselves.

Then came the crucifixion. All their dreams were dashed and slowly crucified. But what success and the realization of all their earthly dreams couldn't accomplish, pain, loss, and reorienting their viewpoint did.

And this process has been going on in the disciples of Jesus ever since. That pain, far from destroying them, did indeed conform them to the image of His Son. The will of God was realized, painful as it was.

I have experienced any number of disappointments and what I would call failures in my life. I have experienced disappointment with God as rungs have broken that I had felt would hold me up. I have experienced the terror of "free-falling" from what I perceived to be the will of God.

In retrospect I have seen that I was not falling out of the will of God; nor had God sadistically pulled the rung out from under me just as I placed my weight on it. My pain was the result of the intense weight and pressure of all my ambitions and dreams being thrust upon a rung that wasn't there. In fact, the ladder wasn't even there. I experienced the sensation of having the spiritual wind knocked out of me.

No, life simply hadn't turned out the way I was sure God should have planned it. He wasn't following my script! But He was faithfully involved in doing what He had promised all along He would do. He was conforming me to the image of Christ.

When I enter heaven it will not be as pastor and author Dan Schaeffer. All my trophies, plaques, successes, and accomplishments will fade away, and my progress in that conformity to the image of Christ will take center stage. Only then will I see clearly how it had always been center stage.

Our life here is a classroom where the subject is transformation, and the goal conformation. If we can come to understand that, we will be more prepared and understanding of pain, loss, and disappointment when it comes. Our greatest disappointment with God is a result of our feeling that God simply isn't keeping His promises to us. He didn't do what we thought we heard Him saying He would.

But God is keeping His promises to us. He never promised us wealth, health, or perpetual happiness. Scripture is replete with examples of just the opposite. He has promised to make us the eternal objects of His love, and conform us into the image of His beloved Son. This is God's will!

The will of God shouldn't be thought of as a ladder where we are constantly reaching for the next set of rungs of happiness or accomplishment, but a slow, persistent, and determined process, or journey, by which God is allowing different experiences, both pleasant and unpleasant, to shape our lives.

PAINFUL CHARACTER SHAPERS

Does God have certain experiences and accomplishments and tasks He wants us to achieve? Certainly, and Scripture demonstrates that God prepares people for different ministries and works (Ephesians 2:1–10). These pleasant moments of achievement and experience are also a valuable aspect of conforming us to the image of Christ.

But they are only part of the process. Happiness, achievement, and accomplishment are never, of themselves, enough to conform us to the image of God's Son.

The problem is that we don't conform unless heat is applied to our lives. We are stiff and stubborn and inflexible. Human success does not soften us; it often hardens us to God's efforts to change us. But failure, loss, pain, trouble: these are tremendous shapers of character. These things loosen stiff necks and bend proud knees.

Success can be a very false guide. If you think about it, Hitler was successful most of his career; so was Stalin and Lenin and any number of cruel tyrants. Remember our definition of success: "To obtain a desired object or end"? Using this as a definition, they were eminently successful in many areas, because they obtained their desired end.

There are moments of pressure when we feel we absolutely must know the will of God, right now! Why? Because of our fear of failure, or our dread over the prospect that our deepest desires won't come to pass. Interestingly, Webster's defines *failure* as "a lack of success." We are scared stiff we aren't going to get what we want, and that is what we are focused on, *getting what we want*.

But human success will not always be the will of God for our lives, because it finds its source in our desires. Our desires find their source in our hearts, and our hearts are deceitfully wicked, says the Lord, and not to be trusted.

"The heart is more deceitful than all else and is desperately sick; who can understand it?" (Jeremiah 17:9).

Human success means we get or accomplish what we desire; real success is achieved when we accomplish what God desires. Therefore, we can encounter loss, failure, pain, opposition, persecution, and more, and yet be smack-dab in the middle of God's perfect will for our lives.

While we see only the difficulty of the moment, God sees the effectiveness of the process. When we look more like Jesus, more conformed to the image of His Son *after* an experience than we were before, we are successful. It is frequently true that we look and act less and less like Christ after human success, when our ego and pride get stroked, than we do after the results of failure have had their impact on us.

Jesus' death on the cross turned our human understanding of success upside down.

- He was abandoned by His followers at the end of three years of intense ministry with them
- He was betrayed by one of His own twelve disciples
- His popularity plummeted in a week's time
- He died a criminal death, penniless and stigmatized

Everything that we would define as failure spelled success to Him. He said that He had come to give His life a ransom for many, and that never made sense to the human-success-oriented disciples, so they weren't able to come to grips with His death. To them, it had to be failure, loss, a horrible mistake. It would have been a fool's errand to have tried to convince any of them that the crucifixion of Christ was the perfect will of God for Jesus, furthermore, and that it was the perfect will of God for them. Jesus' disciples are still having problems with this issue.

GOD'S PROMISE AND OUR DREAMS

God has not promised to subsidize our dreams, only to fulfill His will, which is good and perfect toward us, even though we can't always see the good and perfect part of it while we're in the middle of the process that will bring about His will.

When we say we are seeking God's will, what we often mean is that we want God to submit to *our* will. To truly seek God's will, true spiritual success, is to come to terms with our true condition.

We think we have a few rough edges here and there, but we're mostly smooth. The reality is that we're mostly rough, with only small evidences of smoothness in our lives. The difficult truth is that we need painful, character-shaping experiences more than blue ribbons, trophies, awards, and a "happily ever after" life.

Maybe you're presently seeking God's will for some area in your life. Take a moment and ask yourself a hard question. What am I really seeking? Am I seeking to avoid all the unpleasantness of life? Am I trying to detour pain, loss, opposition, and persecution by seeking the will of God? Am I using the will of God like a talisman, to bring good luck?

Are we willing to exchange our definitions of success with God's and then pray for His will? We are to imitate Christ who said to the Father, "Not my will, but Thy will be done."

Can we begin to pray this way? "Lord, I pray for Your will in my

- relationships
- health
- job
- dreams
- family
- and aspirations

even if it does not meet all my human desires. Help me to achieve all my aspirations that fit into Your will, and to accept Your will for those that do not. Help me to become more like my Lord, even when it is painful."

Yes, painful. There are pains in life, and some are self-imposed. We sometimes have ignored the clear will of God with the hopes that we can take a shortcut. But what happens when we actually go out of bounds? Once out of bounds, always out of bounds: is that the rule? What happens when we take determined detours from the will of God? Let's take a look.

FOLLOW THROUGH

1. Have I ever consciously or unconsciously thought that if I could just find God's will for my life, I would be successful? How did I develop this thinking?

2. I have always defined personal success as

3. I have at times sought the will of God for my life with the hope that if I found it, nothing would ever go wrong. (True or false. Why?)

4. Can I think of a time when the unmistakable will of God for me was

misfortune	loss
failure	persecution
pain	shame
opposition	embarrassment

   (Choose one or two and discuss.)

5. "Human failure is often God's success." Why can this be such a frightening truth in my life?

6. The last time I found myself to be "successful" but *not* in the will of God was when

7. Reread Romans 8:29 and list as many ways as you can to be "conformed to the image of His Son." Spend some time dealing with the ramifications of these different issues.

8. What are some of my natural human reactions to success? To failure? How could both of them be used to lead me away from God?

Making Contact

In a quiet moment of reflection, purpose to redefine success in your heart and life. Ask God to help you be sensitive to the Holy Spirit during this process. This could drastically change the direction and tenor of your life, so also ask for more courage. Write down as best you can your new definition of success and put it in the places you see it most often. Commit to memory Romans 8:29: "For those whom He foreknew, He also predestined to become conformed to the image of His Son, so that He would be the firstborn among many brethren." The next time you struggle with real success, bring this verse back to your mind and heart and let God speak to you again.

CHAPTER TEN

Out of Bounds:
Detours from the Will of God

One road leads home
and a thousand lead into the wilderness.

—C. S. Lewis[20]

One pressing question we must deal with as we delve deeper into the subject of God's will is this: What happens when, by my own actions, I leave the path of God's perfect will for my life?

Now this question assumes that there is a perfect will for our lives. Not only a perfect moral will, revealed in Scripture, but also a sovereign providential will that deals specifically with *my* future, with *your* future. I am convinced that there is a perfect providential will for each life, and that we can, by our own sin, detour from that path.

I should stop for a moment and say that there are those who disagree. Some fine Christian men and women argue that we are guided only by God's moral will. In other matters God is not interested in which choices we make. For example, God does not care who I marry, where I choose to live, where I go to college, or what vocation I choose. In these non-moral areas we are simply to use godly wisdom in our choices.

I actually agree with much of what they say. God's moral will does guide many, if not most, of my decisions. I don't have to ask God whether or not I should become involved in immorality, or punch my neighbor in the nose, or steal from my employer.

Furthermore, godly wisdom addresses countless issues concerning God's direction in my life. Biblical principles cover far more issues of life than many Christians think. Yet, I draw the line here. I do believe God has a perfect sovereign will for my life, even though that perfect will sometimes involves pain and difficulty. I believe there is certain and specific pain and difficulty He allows in my life that others will not experience, and vice versa. There are also certain places God will lead me, and certain people He wants me to come in contact with, people and places He has not designed for anyone else. This is because what is needed to conform *me* to the image of Christ is different from what someone else might need.

I am convinced of this belief every time I look into the eyes of my children. If God didn't have a specific plan for Dan to marry Annette, then Christi, Andrew, and Katie were coincidental blessings that God didn't plan, but allowed. This is too great a leap for me to make.

Furthermore, the Bible is replete with examples of God's leading of men and women to undertake specific tasks and vocations—the kind of leading that could not be arrived at by relying only on His moral will and wisdom. Was it significant that Joseph chose Mary to be his bride, before the Holy Spirit visited her? Was Joseph thrust into his role through chance and coincidence, or was a sovereign, providential will guiding these events? Was it just happy coincidence that he was of the tribe of Judah, lived in the same area as Mary, and subsequently married her? No, it wasn't simply a matter of moral will or godly wisdom that guided him. There was more to that decision, and the implications were far too important to be left to chance.

I believe that as we obey God's moral will, and apply godly wisdom, He leads us into His providential will, which includes specifics such as vocation, spouse, ministry, where to live, and many other pivotal choices we must make in life.

I firmly believe in the sovereignty of God over the affairs of men. God moves in the shadows of our lives in ways we can't possibly imagine. An in-depth study of the book of Esther in the Old Testament reveals the marvelous divine choreography of God as He works in the shadows of our lives to accomplish His sovereign plan.

He who hears the footsteps of an ant, and watches over the sparrows, and has every hair on our heads counted is far more involved in leading each of us directly into His sovereign plan and will than a moral will and godly wisdom viewpoint alone can account for. Furthermore, the omniscience of God demands that God knows the future. If there is something God doesn't know, He is less than infinite, less than perfect—and that is impossible. If God knows the future, there is a future that is *knowable*, a predetermined plan, as we will see later.

However, having said all that, there is still a mystery to God's will that we must acknowledge. His will certainly incorporates the average and reasonable, but at times He chooses the strange and unpredictable to lead us as well. He keeps His own counsel, and His ways are unsearchable. His ways are higher than our ways, and His thoughts higher than our thoughts (Isaiah 55:9). What we often seek to do is guard ourselves from disappointment or disillusionment when what we thought was going to happen doesn't.

To ease our pain, and "let God off the hook," we simply conclude that God didn't really care what choice we made. I believe He does. We must never let the pain of unrealized expectations lead us to believe that God is somehow standing aloof from the details of life, or uninvolved with leading us every moment. To God there are no "peripheral issues" in our lives.

However, the nagging question remains. Have I, by my own wrong choices, ruined my chances at the happiness God had planned for me? What happens to me, what course does my life take, now that I have detoured from God's will by violating His moral commandments? Maybe I was involved in a divorce in which I was equally responsible for the breakup, or maybe I was involved in promiscuous sex, or addicted to a substance, or was convicted of a crime, or addicted to a habit of sin that has ruined my life. Where do I stand? Is the perfect will of God for my life just a pipe dream now?

This is such an important question for so many, including myself, for we have all violated His moral commands, and turned left when He said turn right. I hope this issue becomes clearer for you through a story I think might help. Just sit back, relax, and listen.

THE ICE PEOPLE

Once upon a time, in a faraway land, lived an old and very kind king. He was a very wealthy king whose kingdom stretched for hundreds of miles in every direction. His fertile lands were filled with orchards and vines and fields that brought forth wonderful vegetation. The fruits and vegetables were unsurpassed, and the animals in the kingdom were healthy and numerous, providing both food and work.

His kingdom was beautiful, filled with softly rolling hills covered with wild green grasses, stately trees, and lovely meadows. The days were mostly filled with warm sunlight and soft breezes. Beautiful brooks meandered through the land, filling small scenic ponds, and beautiful, quiet tree-lined lakes. Yes, the king had everything he could want, and would have died a happy old man, except for one thing. His people were old and dying. There were not enough young people to till the fields and tend the orchards and get married and have children who would laugh and play in the meadows and brooks and lakes. The sound of children's laughter was seldom heard in the king's realm. Much of the fruit and produce of the kingdom rotted, for there were not enough people to eat them. The king became very sad.

Then one day, news came of a people who lived far, far away in a land called the Ice Kingdom. These people lived in a world of cold and ice and darkness. They had to wear heavy, thick coats and blankets to keep warm. The sun rarely appeared there, and when it did, it brought little comfort. They had never tasted fruits or vegetables, for none grew in the Ice Kingdom. Their children rarely played, because life was hard, and it was too cold and dark. They rarely laughed or sang. Their lives were dreary and hard. And there they lived and died, year after year, for they knew nothing of the great old king and his beautiful kingdom.

But one day the good king remembered the Ice People in their distant land, and he quickly sent his most trusted advisor to visit them and persuade them to come and live in his country. The advisor traveled many months to finally reach the Ice Kingdom, for it was a long and difficult journey. When he arrived, he caused quite a commotion, for the Ice People had never seen anyone from outside their kingdom. Many were suspicious of him. But when he arrived, he told them of the great king, and he described his beautiful kingdom to them. He told the Ice People of the king's promise, that he would give to those who journeyed all the way to his palace the best of his lands and orchards and homes.

When the Ice People heard this news, many of them grumbled. Some didn't believe that such a good king could exist, so they ignored the advisor and walked away. Others didn't believe such a place as was being described could exist, so they walked away also. A few even said, "We may have a hard life here, but at least we don't have to answer to any king, so we'll stay where we are." But some of the Ice People wanted to have a good king; they trusted the messenger and accepted the offer gladly. They were tired of the Ice Kingdom and wanted to go where it was warm and beautiful, even though they could not imagine some of the places the king's advisor described.

Finally, the advisor gathered all those who wanted to go and told them that they were to follow a seldom-used path, called the King's Highway, which would eventually lead them straight to the king's palace. He warned them not to take any detours, for if they did, they would surely get lost. Only remaining on the path would ensure their safe arrival.

The advisor soon left and returned to his land. Not long after, the Ice People set out for the new kingdom. It wasn't long before they discovered the partially hidden path the advisor had told them about, one they had never known even existed, and they set out on it. For weeks the Ice People struggled through blizzards and storms to travel over the giant snow mountains that surrounded their homeland; it was not always an easy path. But finally, slowly, the temperature began to get warmer, and they passed over the mountains. The sun came out and they began to feel its warmth, and smiles broke out on their faces. Soon they were able to take off some of their heavier coats, for it wasn't as cold in this part of the country.

With each mile they walked forward the cold was left further behind and they soon began to see the outskirts of the great king's realm, fields and hills covered with wild fruit trees and untamed vines. A few of the Ice People tasted the good food, and it was so much better than anything they had ever eaten; they settled there, for they had grown tired of the long journey. Others kept going, hoping for yet warmer weather and the orchards and cultivated fields they had been promised.

But here and there along the King's Highway were detours, roads leading somewhere unknown. At first no one traveled them, remembering the advisor's warning, but after a while a few took the detours out of curiosity. Perhaps the road was a shortcut, they reasoned. After all, they argued, why take a long journey that is hard if you can find a shortcut? But they ended up lost, and it took much time to find the Highway again.

Later, they found out much to their chagrin that every detour would eventually deposit them back on the Highway, but many miles back from where they had taken the detour. Now they faced making up ground they had already traveled. The weather was colder until they got back on the path again, and again began the journey toward the palace. Others got so lost they never found the Highway again, and eventually settled in the countryside.

However, every person who had come from the Ice Kingdom was glad. Some felt regret they would never see the Great Palace, but the weather was warmer here than they had ever experienced, and the food was more abundant. Life was good. They never regretted leaving the Ice Kingdom nor did they want to return.

Many kept going, stopping and settling further down the road where it was a little warmer and the food was even better. A few brave pilgrims made it all the way to the royal palace where the kind king welcomed them warmly and with great joy, and they entered a land that surpassed anything they had seen before. It was the most beautiful place they could have imagined, and the fruit was sweeter, the vegetables bigger, the trees grander, the meadows greener than anything else along the path. And there they lived happily ever after, the objects of the king's loving attention.

The Ice People in this story are those who do not yet have a relationship with God. The king is God. His palace is His perfect will and plan for each of our lives, and the Highway is the direction we must take to arrive at His will. It is the place He has prepared for us, and wants us to experience. But He allows us to make detours if we choose, and these detours can keep us from ever reaching the ultimate joy God had planned for us.

But even though we may make a detour in life, make decisions outside of His will, we are still in His kingdom, and all progress we make forward takes us into more fulfilling lives than anything we had experienced before. Since we have never known God's perfect providential plan for us, we've never seen the Great Palace, but clearly remember where we were before God saved us, all progress we make in His kingdom is a blessing. We never know what we might have missed, we are only grateful for what we have already received. At any point we can keep traveling closer and closer to the perfect will of God for us, and the closer we get, the more fulfilling it is. But we never have to go back to the Ice Kingdom.

DETOURS AND COVER-UPS

This is just a story, but I hope it helps us understand truths of God's will in our lives. Now, let's look briefly at someone whose life illustrates these truths from Scripture. That person was the great King David. In 2 Samuel 11 we follow the account of an older David. He had ruled many years and was now staying home while his troops went out to war. His life had been one that had stayed on the path of God's will. He had been blessed immeasurably with many honors, riches, wives, homes, and pleasures.

But one day, as he walked on the roof of his royal palace, he spied a beautiful young woman bathing next door. Her name was Bathsheba. He gazed at her, and lusted after her, and then had her brought to him. They committed adultery, and then he sent her back home. In one moment, a lifetime of walking the Royal Highway was halted. David had taken a detour. Later, Bathsheba reported to the king that she was pregnant.

Instead of getting back on the Highway by repenting of his sin, David took another detour to cover his tracks. After discovering Uriah the Hittite was her husband and after trying unsuccessfully to get him to sleep with his wife to cover his sin, David had Uriah put in the front lines of battle, where he was ultimately killed. After Bathsheba had mourned her husband, David married her, and brought her into his home.

God then sent Nathan the prophet to deal with David's detour. I'd like you to hear some of what God had to say to David.

> Nathan then said to David, "You are the man! Thus says the LORD God of Israel, 'It is I who anointed you king over Israel and it is I who delivered you from the hand of Saul. I also gave you your master's house and your master's wives into your care, and I gave you the house of Israel and Judah; and if that had been too little, I would have added to you many more things like these!'" (2 Samuel 12:7–8).

"I would have added to you many more things like these." The future that God had planned for David did not include this detour. Many of the blessings God had in store for David would not materialize because of this detour.

I again want to ask the question, what happens when, by my own actions, I leave the path of God's perfect will? Let's find some of the answers in David's life and in God's dealing with him. I think the first thing we see is that:

Detours from God's Will Have Immediate and Long-term Consequences

The son born to David and Bathsheba through his sin died. This was an immediate and tragic consequence. The long-term consequences are detailed in 2 Samuel 12:10:

> "The sword shall never depart from your house, because you have despised Me and have taken the wife of Uriah the Hittite to be your wife." Thus says the LORD, "Behold, I will raise up evil against you from your own household."

It is instructional to read in Samuel of David's sons, who lost respect for him, and this consequence plagued him to his dying day. These were the natural repercussions of choices he'd made. When we detour from God's will, when we choose to disobey His instructions, we also will experience immediate and long-term consequences. This will happen whether we are Christians or not. They are the result of the order God has created in His moral world, where you reap what you sow. We can be completely forgiven for a sin we commit, like David was, but God does not then cancel out the consequences.

One who is an alcoholic can be forgiven. But liver damage still results, and the ravages of alcohol's effects on the body will remain. Divorced people can and will be forgiven, but they will still lose their spouses, and their families will be injured, sometimes irreparably. One who is convicted of a crime can be forgiven, but must still do the time. Those who are sexually promiscuous will be forgiven, but they may still get a sexually transmitted disease and will mourn their lost purity. These are the natural repercussions of choices we have made. But while there are immediate and long-term consequences:

Detours from God's Will Create a New Set of Directions for Our Lives

Each detour we take leaves us with two options. The first option is to return to the main road; the second is to keep going and hope to find another shortcut. Sin is usually an attempt to meet a legitimate need in an illegitimate way. Let's consider the first option.

Repentance (Midcourse Correction)

Here we recognize the mistake we made, are sorry for it, ask forgiveness, and return to the King's Highway. Sure, we've lost some ground, and we are going to have to live with some consequences of our action, but we're back on the road to blessing again. The blessings of God are found only by operating within His moral will, taking His road. Here we are encouraged by God to make a midcourse correction.

Now let's consider the second option.

Unrepentance (Determined Detour)

This attitude is best described as being sad that something bad happened to me as a result of my sin, but not sorry for what I did. It is remorse, but not repentance. We may regret that we are lost, but not the action that got us lost. We don't regret our actions, just the *consequences* of our actions. Here we tell ourselves that this was just a "slight error in judgment," or "an easy mistake to make," or "just one of those things." We have no sorrow over how we have offended God. This is a determined detour from His will. Unfortunately, until this attitude changes, we will not be able to return to God's perfect will for us, and will cut ourselves off from His richest blessings.

These determined detours are the most tragic. David sinned against God, Bathsheba, and Uriah. But because he repented, made a midcourse correction, he was able to enjoy his fellowship with God again, the relationship was restored, and he was again the recipient of God's blessings. While he still had to endure the consequences of His sins, he did it in the strength that God gave him, and God walked with him through these dark moments. In the end, he was called the friend of God and was blessed by Israel.

Saul, the king before him, never made this midcourse correction, and his life became one long miserable affair, punctuated only by a horrible and all-too-predictable end. Furthermore, a forgiven, repentant Christian, is a wiser, humbler, and more gracious person. True maturity is living with the decisions you've made in life, not running away from them.

All of us have made detours. In the game of life, we've all gone out-of-bounds; we are all playing injured—bandaged and sore. But there is no injury, no sin we can commit, that we can't repent from. And when we do, there is no injury that paralyzes us from Christian service, none! Our actions may take us out-of-bounds at times, but honest, genuine, midcourse correction repentance can put us right back in the game. As God had much left to do with David, He has much left to do with us. And when this happens we learn something very valuable for our future.

What Was Not God's Will Can Nevertheless Be His Instrument for Correction and Blessing

David's sin with Bathsheba, against noble Uriah, was horrible and cruel and selfish. There was nothing redeeming about that act. Yet, after David had fully repented, God did not hold a grudge against him. On the contrary, it was through Bathsheba that David was to have a son named Solomon.

An act that was not God's will, nevertheless became His instrument for correction and blessing. Many of us have experienced this truth. Coming from a broken home, I know this lesson well. My parents' divorce was a sin, but it became an instrument to shape my character and prepare me, in a unique way, for ministry.

So, can I miss God's perfect will for my life? Absolutely, and I am sure in numerous ways I already have. But since I don't know what I have missed, and I am happier now than I have ever been in my life, I have no regrets. I may have missed the very best, but I'm as excited as I can be about the good. While I may never experience all God had for me, I may never reach the palace of the king in that respect, it's warmer here and life today is better than anything I have ever experienced before.

Have you ever considered the incredible grace of God in that He never reveals to us what His absolutely perfect providential will for us is? Knowing that we have a sinful nature, and that our choices would eliminate many of these blessings along the way, causing us to agonize over what might have been, He graciously and mercifully and wisely keeps that information to Himself. God keeps His own counsel.

Because of that, we can focus on our gain, and not on our loss. A growing Christian learns one thing and never lets go of it, ever: What we have gained in Christ is far greater than anything we have lost due to sin. Sometimes it takes a few mistakes before we are able to fully comprehend that reality.

And even David would say the same, I believe. Though his life after the sin was fraught with more difficulties than before, he was better. He was a wiser man, and a better and more compassionate king after that.

Where are you? Are you on the Highway, or off on a detour? You've got two choices: a midcourse correction, or a determined detour. God has wonderful plans for you, even if you've taken a detour, and He has a significant ministry and life waiting for you. What may not have been God's will for you can nevertheless be the instrument He uses to bring great blessing into your life.

If you need a midcourse correction, stop right here and seize the opportunity to make it. In true repentance we are sorry not only about the consequences of our sins, but for the sin itself. We confess our sin (agree with God that what we did was wrong), and don't try to make any excuses (1 John 1:9). As a result we experience full and complete forgiveness. It can be done in a moment.

As we look back over our lives we realize we can often see things much clearer now than we could at the time. Some of God's movements in our lives make far more sense from our perspective in the future than they did at the moment. We see what God was doing, but only in retrospect.

Let's take a look at one last aspect of the search for the will of God, for we're going to discover that sometimes the will of God is found only by looking into the past.

FOLLOW THROUGH

1. In the story of the Ice Kingdom, where would I place myself on the journey? Am I getting warmer or colder?

2. Can I think of a time when I made a detour from my walk of obedience, and then was faced with either making a midcourse correction (repentance) or continuing on in my detour (unrepentance)? What did I choose, and what was the result?

3. Have I ever wondered if God really wanted me back after a determined detour I took? How does the experience of David affect my understanding of His attitude toward me? Read Jeremiah 31:3 and Romans 8:32–39, and discover the nature of God's love.

4. If what was not God's will can nevertheless be God's instrument of correction and blessing, how has God used even disobedience in my life to be an instrument of maturity and growth? What was the greatest lesson I learned?

5. What are some things I know I have lost through disobedience and sin? What are the things I have gained in Christ that can never be lost despite disobedience (John 1:12; 2 Corinthians 5:17; Ephesians 1:3–14)?

Making Contact

It's easy to believe that if you have taken a detour, the joy of fulfillment and blessing have been permanently removed from your life. Yet the Scriptures time and time again share the blessings of repentance, restoration, and renewal. In a few quiet moments ask God to give you the strength and power of Christ to repent and be restored, and He will show you the joy and fulfillment that is available to you today. Meditate on Peter, who failed but became faithful again, and David and Abraham and others whom God used greatly, even after times of failure and weakness.

CHAPTER ELEVEN

An Unknown Itinerary

Not as I will, but as thou wilt. To be able to say these words and truly mean them is the highest point we can ever hope to attain. Then, indeed, we have broken out of time's hard shell to breathe, not its stale air, but the fresh, exhilarating atmosphere of eternity.

—Malcolm Muggeridge[21]

We have said much about the will of God, but we have not discovered any "silver bullets" or surefire, can't-miss methods, guaranteed to enlighten you to the will of God. At least, I hope we haven't, because that wasn't the purpose. There are ways to discover certain aspects of God's will, and to that end I hope this book was helpful.

But, finally, the will of God must not be thought of as a destination in life, the fulfillment of a consuming desire of the heart. It is more than knowing whether to turn right or left, buy or sell, marry or break up. It is more than getting the right job, going to the right school, getting married, having a baby, making lots of money, gaining lots of recognition, or any of the other temporary experiences we might seek.

The goal was to show that the will of God is an ever developing, unfolding, often surprising, sometimes disappointing, but ultimately fulfilling journey. Not something that we arrive at after much consternation and work, but something we are involved in every minute of every day.

The will of God could probably best be described as a long airplane flight that we all must take, with many stopovers and changeovers. But the ultimate itinerary is unknown to us. We aren't told where the stopovers and changeovers are going to be, or what planes we will be flying in.

At times in this journey we may travel in a spartan shuttle plane with no amenities. It will be cramped, uncomfortable, and unpleasant, and the passengers next to us may be unfriendly and obnoxious. Sometimes we feel we will take the whole journey in this craft. We dream of flying in a bigger, more comfortable plane, with a different crowd of people.

Then, often without notice, the plane lands, and we are changed over to a different plane, a spacious 767, where we get to ride first-class, sitting next to a more refined and pleasant crowd of people. There is good food, friendly flight attendants to cater to us, jovial conversation with happy travelers, movies, and other creature comforts. We relax, feeling we have finally arrived, and get comfortable because the journey is wonderful in this new plane.

Since this is what we always dreamed of, we settle in thinking this is the way it's always going to be. Until, to our utter amazement, our plane lands again, and we are transferred to an aging WWII cargo plane with no amenities, movies, food, attendants—no creature comforts of any kind.

And we may finish our journey on this plane, or our flight may be one that is rather short-lived, after which we are then deposited into a huge 767 with all the luxuries. On the other hand, we may be shown to a small aging two-seater Cessna, flying right into a storm, or anything between these extremes. We never know; we're never told beforehand.

I have met Christian men and women who make lifelong plans for certain desired ends—the long-awaited flight aboard the 767. He may describe it as God's will for him; she might call it the fulfillment of her heart's desire. Sometimes they arrive at it, whether it be a vocation, a lifestyle, marital status, parenthood, a full-time ministry, or a myriad of other dreams.

Of those who arrive, some get to take the whole flight of life in that plane, but others get only a short ride, and then are unexpectedly handed another stopover in life, and a dramatic change of scenery. They may never get to ride that 767 again, because their flight was short. Some people will never get to experience the inside of those comfortable planes.

But it is not because God is some sort of sadistic fiend, it is because His focus is on something more important than the mode of travel. He has His eyes on the process, on our transformation. God knows what flights will transform us, and in what order, which is why He chooses our itinerary for us. He is not preparing us for the next 100 years, He is preparing us for eternity.

Ironically, on any plane, any type you can mention, whether it's an aging dilapidated cargo plane or the Concorde SST, you will find people who enjoy the ride, people who endure the ride with complaining, and some folks who are absolutely miserable. This will hold true regardless of the plane they are in at the time.

Our itinerary in life is unknown to us, but not to God. To get to our final destination, "conformed to the image of His Son," we all require different flight experiences. There will be some 707, and maybe even some 767 flights in our lives, but there will also be some broken-down cargo plane experiences, and everything between. These are not accidents, or errors, but the result of a thoughtful itinerary scheduled by God.

For the first years of his life, Moses was flying in a 767, hobnobbing with the upper crust. Then there was a planned stopover, and Moses was shown to a dilapidated cargo plane for the next forty years. Later there was another stopover, and he took the rest of his flight in another plane. He never rode in the 767 again, because it would not have aided in the process of conforming him to the image of God.

David's life started out in a cargo plane, but then he had a stopover to board a 767 as king of Israel. Several times in life he experienced stopovers and changeovers. He lost his kingdom, became a refugee because of his rebellious son, and then gained it back. David needed all those stopovers and changeovers, and so do we.

Peter was a simple fisherman leading a quiet life. When Christ called him, he left that simple life and became a disciple who experienced both honor and shame, exaltation and desperate fear. Then after the death and resurrection of Christ, he became a great leader. But his life ends in a plane wreck, as he is martyred for his faith.

When, might we ask, were Moses, David, and Peter experiencing the will of God for their lives? It was at each stopover, and in each new plane. The will of God was the journey.

The will of God is not just the fulfillment of our temporary longing or desire, it is the divine itinerary of our life in which we learn to follow His moral instruction, which gets us to the proper planes, and then to trust His divine itinerary for our lives, whatever mode of transportation may be required.

Coming to terms with this is freeing. You are finally able to come up with an honest and biblical definition of success. It is not a first-class, 767 existence where life is always pleasant and comfortable, our names in lights, our bank accounts full, our health perfect, and our lives the envy of our peers. Success is the willingness and faithfulness to get on whatever flight God has booked for us. It is the desire to take whatever route may be required to conform us to the image of His Son—whether it involves a smooth flight or prolonged turbulence.

It is, finally, prizing that goal over and above an easier ride through life if that's what it takes. It is knowing that at times, an apparent step down or back in life, is in God's itinerary, really a step forward in your transformation.

LIFE IS SHORT

In a church I used to pastor is a man I greatly admire. A few years ago he learned he has a debilitating disease. He sought a cure, but there was none. He sought biblical healing through the biblical formula found in James 5:14–15. Prayers of great faith were lifted up, but God's answer was no, the disease would remain.

This was a planned stopover for him and his family. At a Thanksgiving service I asked him and a number of other people to get up and share what they were thankful for. He agreed to speak.

He went up to the microphone and shared simply, quietly, and briefly about his physical condition, and then after a few more short thoughts, closed with words that I will never forget. It is a scene that still brings a lump to my throat.

With a wavering voice he reminded us of a truth that had recently become prominent in his life: "Life is so short, and eternity is so long," he said. With that he walked back to his seat and sat down. You could have heard a pin drop in that room. Now, I had said that same thing over and over again in sermon after sermon, but never was that truth driven home more powerfully than it was through that man's testimony. He not only knew the truth; he was living it.

He was more like Jesus now than before, and as a result, we became more like Jesus than we were before. Could we view our financial struggles in the same light again? Was it such a tragic disappointment to be unable to step up to a higher lifestyle? Many of our consuming passions were put into perspective by one short sentence spoken by a man being powerfully conformed to the image of his Savior.

He realized, and he helped us realize, that our Christian lives are simply journeys where we are undergoing the process of transformation. We will have pleasant stopovers and comfortable flights, and we will encounter some turbulence and unpleasant experiences. But the good and the bad are both vitally necessary to our individual sanctification. And so, for you and for me, the journey continues.

Be thou a bright flame before me,
Be thou a guiding star above me,
Be thou a smooth path below me,
And be a kindly shepherd behind me,
Today, tonight, and forever.

—Alexander Carmichael[22]

FOLLOW THROUGH

1. The plane ride I'm on could best be described as

2. The transformation that God is working in me that I can see is

3. "Success is the willingness and faithfulness to get on whatever flight God has booked for us." How comfortable am I becoming with this idea? What do I still struggle with?

4. Have I ever experienced a time when a step back in my life was actually a step forward in my transformation?

Making Contact

Take out your original letter to God (see chapter 1, Making Contact) asking Him what you most needed and wanted out of this study. How many of your questions were answered? How many still remain? Do you still need to know all the answers?

Write down what you have learned that will benefit you in the future, and what is already beginning to benefit you now. What was the most important lesson you took away from this study?

NOTES

[1] Harvey Mackay, "If at First You Do Succeed—Watch It," *Orange County Register* (September 25, 1995), 9.

[2] Edyth Draper, *Draper's Quotations for the Christian World* (Wheaton: Tyndale House, 1992), #8087.

[3] *Draper's* #5392.

[4] *Draper's* #5454.

[5] C. S. Lewis, *The Discarded Image* (Cambridge, U. K.: Cambridge University Press, 1964), 176.

[6] Quoted in John Bartlett, *Bartlett's Familiar Quotations,* ed. Justin Kaplan (Boston: Little, Brown and Co.), 620.

[7] Elisabeth Elliot, *A Slow and Certain Light* (Nashville: Abingdon Press, 1982).

[8] *Draper's* #5420.

[9] *Draper's* #5445.

[10] *Draper's* #5435.

[11] *Draper's* #5371.

[12] *The Letters of C. S. Lewis to Arthur Greeves (1914–1965),* ed. Walter Hooper (New York: Collier/Macmillan, 1960), 243.

[13] *Draper's* #5423.

[14] *Draper's* #5461.

[15] *Letters of C. S Lewis,* 225.

[16] C. S. Lewis, *The World's Last Night and Other Essays* (New York: Harcourt Brace Jovanovich, 1960), 109.

[17] *Draper's* #4015.

[18] *Draper's* #3051.

[19] Joseph Ton, "Living Sacrifice," *Leadership Magazine*, Fall 1987, 44.

[20] C. S. Lewis, *The Pilgrim's Regress* (Grand Rapids, Mich.: Eerdman's, 1958), 155.

[21] *Draper's,* #4976.

[22] *Draper's,* #5375.

NOTE TO THE READER

The publisher invites you to share your response to the message of this book by writing Discovery House Publishers, Box 3566, Grand Rapids, MI 49501, USA. For information about other Discovery House books, music, DVDs, or videos, contact us at the same address or call 1-800-653-8333. Find us on the Internet at http://www.dhp.org/ or send e-mail to books@dhp.org.

Dan Schaeffer invites you to contact him through his Web site: www.danschaeffer.com.